LOWE'S®
Improving Home Improvement®

decorating with
paint & color

welcome to a world of color

PAINT OFFERS A WORLD OF WAYS TO UPDATE AND ENLIVEN ANY INTERIOR, whether you use a single color, a combination of colors, or a decorative technique like colorwashing, combing, or faux wood graining. The challenge is to determine the best approach for your home, and this takes some planning. In this book, Lowe's brings you everything you need to know about color and paint, the tools you'll use, and how to use them, as well as guidelines to help you combine colors creatively. You'll find special techniques for grand effects as well as quick, easy projects that will spruce up your home without breaking the bank or requiring lots of skill and time.

Lowe's Decorating with Paint & Color joins our growing series: **Complete Home Improvement and Repair**, **Complete Landscaping**, **Complete Home Decorating**, **Complete Kitchen**, **Complete Bathroom**, and **Creative Ideas for Outdoor Living.** They're all part of our commitment to providing you with ideas, information, and inspiration, along with the right tools, materials, fixtures, and finishes, for every one of your home improvement projects.

Lowe's Decorating with Paint & Color is the result of a close collaboration with two of our valued vendor partners—Valspar Corporation and Olympic Paints. Their expertise joins with ours to bring you up-to-date information, innovative projects, and beautiful photographs showcasing the latest in color trends and decorative techniques. As you put the ideas in this book to work, consult Lowe's Paint Sales Specialists on the best choice of colors, paints, primers, finishes, and tools to make your project a success. And for even more information, take advantage of our in-store do-it-yourself clinics and the helpful how-to library at www.lowes.com.

Lowe's has a long, proud tradition of helping its customers create beautiful homes. For painting projects you can be proud of, let us be your guide.

LOWE'S®
Improving Home Improvement®

Lowe's Companies, Inc.

Bob Tillman
CHAIRMAN AND CEO

Robert Niblock
PRESIDENT

Melissa S. Birdsong
DIRECTOR, TREND
FORECASTING & DESIGN

Zach Miller
MERCHANDISER

Bob Gfeller
SENIOR VP, MARKETING

Jean Melton
VP, MERCHANDISING

Mike Menser
SENIOR VP, GENERAL
MERCHANDISE MANAGER

Dale Pond
SENIOR EXECUTIVE VP,
MERCHANDISING

Ann Serafin
MERCHANDISING DIRECTOR

table of contents

Lowe's Series
PROJECT DIRECTOR René Klein

Staff for Lowe's Decorating with Paint & Color
EDITOR Sally W. Smith

DESIGN AND PRODUCTION
Hespenheide Design

WRITER Lisa Stockwell Kessler

TEXT EDITOR Esther Ferington

PREPRESS COORDINATOR
Eligio Hernandez

PROOFREADER Alicia Eckley

INDEXER Nanette Cardon

PRODUCTION DIRECTOR
Lory Day

DIGITAL PRODUCTION
Jeff Curtis/Leisure Arts

The Valspar Corporation
Randy Schuetz
GENERAL MERCHANDISE MANAGER

Brooke Smith
GRAPHIC DESIGN/
MARKETING MANAGER

Holly Seese
MARKETING SERVICES MANAGER

Olympic Paints/PPG Industries
Kathy Boytim
MARKETING MANAGER
NATIONAL ACCOUNTS

Kathy Quirin
MARKETING SUPERVISOR

On the cover
Photograph by Philip Harvey. Interior design by Nestor D. Matthews/
Matthews Studio. *Color Matches* Bedroom wall: American Tradition Lilac
Moon; trim: American Tradition Ultra White; hallway wall: Alexander Julian
At Home Dolphin.

COVER DESIGN Vasken Guiragossian

Page 1: Photo furnished by Olympic Paints. Wall: Olympic's #221-6,
Broomstick.

Page 2: Photo furnished by Valspar. Walls: Eddie Bauer Home Meadow;
trim: Eddie Bauer Home Honeysuckle Bloom.

10 9 8 7 6 5 4 3 2
First printing October 2003

how to use this book

PAINTING AND COLOR PROJECTS CAN be as simple or as ambitious as you choose. With paint, you can transform your whole house, add character to a room, or revitalize a single piece of furniture. You can do it all at once or in small steps, depending on the time and finances you have available.

Whether you want advice on selecting paints and colors, do-it-yourself instructions for repairing walls and painting rooms, or step-by-step information on the latest decorative painting techniques and projects for walls or furnishings, you've come to the right place. Here's a preview of what you can find in the chapters ahead.

Photographs throughout the book illustrate exciting ideas for decorating with color and paint.

all about color

This chapter begins with basics—including the decorator's central color tool, the color wheel—and gives plenty of examples of how to put together color combinations successfully. It discusses how color can alter the mood and even the perceived shape of a room. Finally, it examines how light, contrast, texture, and pattern can affect a color scheme. Throughout this chapter, photos offer inspiration and illustrate guidelines for creating color schemes. The information here will help direct you toward the color choices that are right for you.

color in your home

Narrowing the choices among the colors you like can be a challenge. This chapter includes a list of practical considerations— from the architectural style of your home and how a room is used to the furnishings in the room and the subtle differences created by different lighting sources—all of them amply illustrated. The chapter also covers design elements, including special decorative effects you can create with paint.

painting tools and techniques

This chapter offers the meat and bones of the painting process, including the essential tools and materials you'll use to

More than 50 projects offer a wealth of choices for interesting, colorful effects. See pages 164–165 for instructions on creating this brushed-metal finish.

paint walls and trim, as well as specialty tools for decorative painting techniques. There's information on the best way to prepare a room for painting, as well as how to repair walls, apply the paint, clean up, and dispose of any hazardous materials.

Whether you're a painting novice or an experienced do-it-yourselfer, you'll find tips and shortcuts here to save time and prevent mistakes.

simple **paint** projects

Take a look at this chapter for fast and easy creative paint projects to spruce up a room with color. Most projects can be completed in less than a day and require little or no previous experience with a paintbrush. Illustrated with step-by-step photography, they range from painting an unfinished wood chair to altering a room's apparent dimensions with clever use of color on one or more walls. You'll also find pages of stencil and stamp patterns that you can use or adapt to create your own wall patterns.

decorative **effects** for walls

If you are comfortable working with paint and want to add more texture or pattern to your walls, try one of the projects in this chapter. Presented in the same step-by-step

style, they cover almost every decorative painting technique used today, from combing to dragging, ragging to spattering, and more. You can stick with a single technique, or combine several techniques for added depth and character.

decorative **effects** for furnishings and woodwork

Walls and ceilings aren't the only painting projects in this book. This chapter starts with instructions on how to prepare wood surfaces—old or new—for painting, then continues through a visual feast of options for furniture, cabinetry, and woodwork. Some use painting techniques inspired by those usually applied to walls, while others deploy faux-finish techniques that create the look of marble, wood grain, or malachite. And when nothing but gilding will do, this section explains how to make your trim or accessories glisten like gold.

Throughout the book, you'll find photographs and illustrations that offer easy step-by-step guidance as well as a wealth of colorful ideas. Specialty products such as Valspar's Decorative Effects paints are highlighted. Lowe's Safety Tips add important safety information, and Lowe's Quick Tips provide nuggets of useful shortcuts and professional advice.

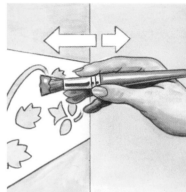

Illustrations, photographs, and step-by-step directions make each technique clear.

LOWE'S QUICK TIP

Tip boxes in the margins offer time-savers and helpful ideas.

all about color

PAINT CAN REVITALIZE ALMOST ANYTHING IN YOUR HOUSE, from walls, ceilings, and floors to furnishings and accessories. The easiest way to decorate a room, paint is often the most economical as well. It is also one of the best ways to add individuality to a home. But, while the process of painting is relatively simple, selecting the right color can be downright intimidating.

This chapter takes the mystery out of working with color, providing you with specific, easy-to-follow guidelines and plenty of visually stunning real-life examples. We start with an introduction to color basics—including the color wheel, a useful tool for determining how well colors work together.

Color does not exist in isolation. When you plan a change in a room, you'll need to consider what's already there. We'll help you evaluate the room's colors and tones, as well as how both natural and artificial light can alter a color's vibrancy. We discuss the psychological values of colors, which affect the mood and livability of a room—knowledge of the very real effects of colors as different as blue and yellow can save you from creating a room that has the right style but the wrong atmosphere for the way you live. Finally, this chapter explores how you can use pattern and texture to add to a room's visual character.

With the information in this chapter, you'll learn to create schemes that work and fix those that don't. More important, you'll be able to use color to develop your own personal style, working with the assurance that you'll be happy with the results.

color basics

SOME PEOPLE HAVE AN INTUITIVE SENSE OF WHICH COLORS WILL WORK WELL together. The rest of us find comfort in the fact there are guidelines. Understanding color and learning to apply color theory is easier once you learn how to use the color wheel (see pages 12–15). To begin, you need to know a few basic terms. They'll help in understanding the color wheel, and in talking with paint sales staff and decorators.

hue

Hue is just another word for color. From the deepest midnight blue and forest green to the softest tones of coral and wheat, all the colors you can imagine are hues. The term "hue," a favorite of the art and design world, is used interchangeably with the word "color."

value

Value refers to the lightness or darkness of a color. There are infinite variations in value, from the palest lights to darks that appear almost black. Value is determined by the amount of white, gray, or black that is added to a pure color.

While it is easiest—and usually best—to think of colors as being light, medium, or dark in value, you'll also hear the terms "tint," "shade," and "tone" used to describe color values. Tints are colors to which white has been added. They are the lighter values, such as pink. Shades are colors that have had black added to them, such as midnight blue, and are darker in value. Tones are colors with gray added; they are usually duller than tints or shades. The process of making tints, shades, or tones from a pure color is called "extending" it. In other words, you extend the number of possibilities for that hue.

intensity

Intensity measures the purity or brightness of a color. Pure, high-intensity colors are easy to spot due to their brilliance. Think of lacquer red, cobalt blue, and taxi-cab yellow, versus less-intense burgundy, navy, and gold. It's easy to confuse intensity and value, but they are not the same. When you look at a color, first ask yourself, "Is it light, medium, or dark?" That's the value. Then ask "Is it bright or dull?" That's the intensity.

Color Matches **Back walls: Laura Ashley Home Old Rose 5; far left wall: American Tradition Jonquil Yellow; shelving: American Tradition Regatta Blue**

Color reigns in this cheerful kitchen nook. The pink wall color, low in both value and intensity, is bordered by intense primaries.

Color intensity helps set a mood. A more intense color can be fresh and stimulating, while low-intensity variations of the same color tend to be quieter and more subdued. Because full-intensity color is so vivid, it is usually used as an accent rather than as the dominant color in a design scheme.

temperature

In the design world, colors are considered to be either warm or cool. Yellows, reds, and oranges seem warm. They are the colors of fire and the sun. The cool colors— greens, blues, and violets—evoke water and nature. Within each group, some colors are referred to as "bridging" colors because each contains both a warm and cool hue. Green is made up of warm yellow and cool blue. Violet is made up of warm red and cool blue. See page 22 to learn how color temperature affects perceptions of the space in a room.

Color Matches (Nickelodeon colors)
Walls: Orange Fusion; trim: Pineapple Paradise; ceiling: Sandtable Yellow

Full-intensity orange and yellow are warm colors that cheer up a room instantly. The cobalt blue pendant lamp is a perfect complement to the color scheme.

A light lavender—Lowe's Earth Elements Whimsy— contains just enough red to keep this room from feeling chilly. It's a great color for a room that gets bright sunlight.

the color wheel

WHEN LIGHT PASSES THROUGH A PRISM, IT SEPARATES INTO A CONTINUOUS range of wavelengths that we perceive as 12 colors. In the color wheel, that sequence of colors is arranged around a circle so you can see how best to put various combinations together. The 12 colors fall into three categories—primary, secondary, and intermediate—that are explained on the following pages. The version of the color wheel illustrated on page 9 uses inner rings to show different values for each pure color. This lets you visualize, for instance, that peach is a tint of orange and that turquoise is a tint of blue-green. A wheel you can purchase is shown below.

Once you have become familiar with the color wheel, you'll find it is easy to select successful color relationships—from safe to audacious—to develop your own design scheme.

This color wheel tool helps you select color combinations with a turn of the inside dial. These wheels are available from the Color Wheel Company, 541/929-7526, or www.colorwheelco.com.

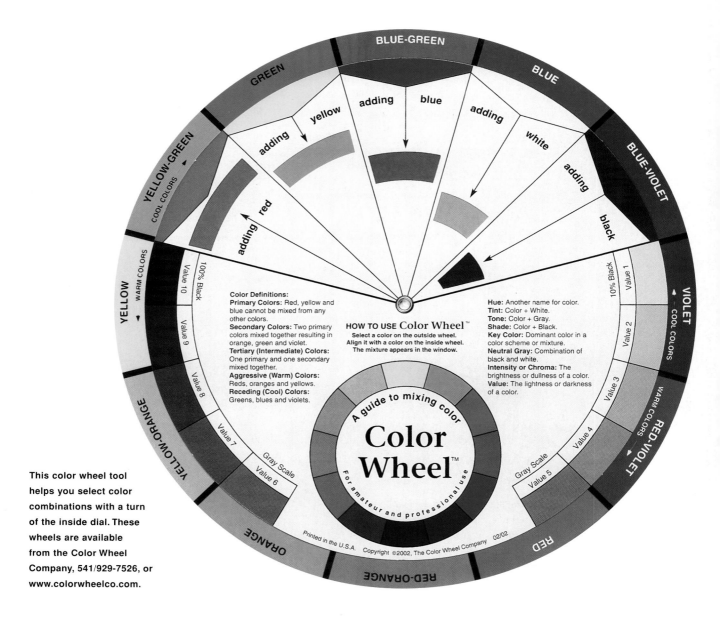

primary colors

Red, blue, and yellow are the primary colors—they cannot be created by combining other colors. When mixed together in different combinations and proportions, they make up all the other colors. Intense primaries in large quantities can be harsh; lower-intensity variations are easier to live with.

secondary colors

When equal parts of two primary colors are combined, the result is a secondary color. Green comes from mixing blue and yellow; orange comes from yellow and red; and violet (often called purple) comes from red and blue. The three secondary colors lie midway between the primary colors on the color wheel.

LOWE'S QUICK TIP

Intense hues from around the color wheel work well together when you vary either their intensities or values or use them in different proportions. If walls are fuchsia, for example, paint your trim a bright teal and add small accents of orange-yellow around the room.

Color Matches (American Tradition colors) Shelving: Harvest Blue; back wall: White

Color Matches (American Tradition colors) Back wall: Vivace Orange; left wall and ceiling: Pale Copper

Above: Full-intensity primaries are most effective when used in unequal quantities. Here blue dominates, while yellow and red provide accents.

Right: Undiluted, the secondary color orange can be brash, but in lower intensities and values, it is an earth color that blends well with furnishings made from wood, stone, and metal.

intermediate colors

When a primary color is mixed with a secondary color, an intermediate color is formed. For instance, blue and green, when mixed, become blue-green. There are six intermediate colors.

tertiary and quaternary colors

Subtle blends of pure color, tertiary and quaternary colors are not represented on the standard color wheel because of limited space. They're richer than shades, tints, or tones, however, and add sophistication and depth to a color scheme.

Tertiary colors are formed by mixing two secondary colors. Orange and green, for instance, create wheat; violet and orange create brick; and violet and green create slate.

By mixing two tertiary colors, you can add quaternary colors to the palette. For example, brick and wheat together form sandstone. Sandstone, juniper, and eggplant are all quaternary colors that are used successfully in interior design.

Red-violet, an intermediate not frequently used to cover walls, is paired here with a tone of yellow in the niches. Lowe's Earth Elements Red Ash is on the walls, with Eclipse in the niches.

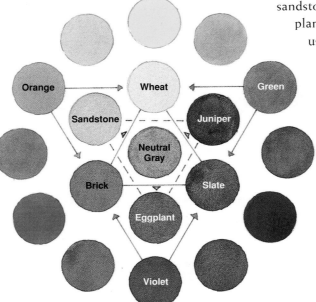

Tertiary and quaternary colors—shown in the inner circle—are rich hues that are easy to live with.

complementary colors

Any two colors that lie opposite each other on the color wheel are complementary. When mixed in equal amounts, such colors neutralize each other, forming a flat gray. By adding a small amount of a color to its complement, you can create a pleasing, less intense version of the predominant color called a complement tint.

non-colors: black, white, and gray

The true neutrals—black, white, and gray—are not found on the color wheel. However, these "non-colors" play an important role in decorating because they can work alone or provide visual relief in a scheme with color, without altering the color relationships.

Below: Neutral cream walls and a golden wood countertop add a touch of warmth to a crisp black and white kitchen.

Color Matches Walls: base coat: Valspar Translucent Cream; glaze : Decorative Effects Burnt Sienna; over stove and back wall of shelving: American Tradition Napoleon Blue

Above: In a complementary color scheme, a blue-violet stove hood is set off against a subtle yellow-orange color-washed wall.

Color Matches Walls: Laura Ashley Home Deep Cowslip 4; cabinets and trim: Valspar Pudding

color combinations

SUCCESSFUL COLOR SCHEMES FALL INTO FOUR BASIC CATEGORIES, RANGING from very subtle to extremely colorful. (See page 21 for a fifth option—technically not a "color" scheme—based on black, white, or gray.) Once you see how the different schemes are formed, you can build your own combinations from a favorite color, adding other colors you love or finding new ones you never considered.

In general, when you work with more than a single color, make one dominant and use the others to enrich the scheme. And remember, you don't have to think of colors in their full intensities.

Using three different values of blue from Lowe's Alexander Julian Pacific Blues of Baja collection, this monochromatic living room is harmonious yet lively. The draperies, rug, and sofa cushions add texture, pattern, and accent colors.

the **monochromatic** scheme

A monochromatic scheme uses variations in value and intensity of a single color to create a virtually fool-proof design scheme. These combinations are both elegant and restful. Imagine walls and furnishings cov-

ered in varying values, and perhaps some patterns, of orange, from peach to burnt umber. Because the colors all come from one source on the color wheel, such rooms have a pleasing unity.

With a monochromatic scheme, too much contrast between values can look uneven. Choose a trim color only a shade or two darker than the wall, or use other

Neutrals in shades of tan, camel, silver, and cream contribute low-key color to a refined living room.

Color Matches (Earth Elements colors)
Walls: Sand Drift; trim and ceiling: Waft

elements to provide a middle value. For instance, if you paint the wall a light blue and the trim slate blue, unify the two colors by selecting upholstery that's between the two in value. You can enliven any monochromatic scheme with texture and pattern, or add interest with a splash of accent color chosen using one of the other three color schemes, such as an antiqued red chest in an ochre room.

The easiest way to build a monochromatic paint scheme is to select colors from paint charts or chips that include several values of the same color.

neutral colors

One of the most refined monochromatic schemes combines neutral colors. Unlike the true neutrals—white, black, and gray—these "colorized" neutrals are very low-intensity versions of colors. Take green to its lowest intensity and the result is a neutral. Yellow becomes a buttery off-white. Neutrals can vary in value, just like any other colors. Pearl and butter are light in value; celery and camel are medium; coffee bean and charcoal are dark.

These softer hues lend ambience and a hint of color to a room but never overwhelm it or stand out. They are ideal backgrounds for furnishings and artwork, since they put the focus on what's in the room, not what color is on the walls. Use the color wheel to discover the most pleasing partners for these colors. For a complementary contrast to a neutral yellow-green, you might choose merlot, a very low-intensity red-violet that lies opposite yellow-green on the wheel.

The wall color in this sophisticated bedroom is a warm neutral from Lowe's Waverly Home Classics called Natural. White trim and black furnishings provide contrast, while the black and white bedcover introduces pattern.

analogous schemes

Combinations of "analogous" or related colors use colors that lie side by side on the color wheel, producing a harmonious effect. Red, red-orange, and orange are analogous, and so are blue, blue-violet, and violet. The key to an analogous scheme is a common color. In the first example, it's red (orange is half red). In the second, it's blue (violet is half blue). These examples demonstrate the most agreeable analogous combinations: those that include one primary and the secondary and intermediate colors that fall to one side of it.

As with a monochromatic combination, an analogous scheme gains interest from a lively mix of patterns, textures, and finishes. To avoid monotony, you can vary the quantities of the colors and make one an intense accent. Wood, art, and accessories can add impact as well.

Blue and blue-green set a cool mood in a kitchen. A bit of white trim is welcome in this analogous scheme.

Color Matches **(American Tradition colors) Wall: Riverside; cabinet: Monet Blue; trim: White Peony**

Yellow walls soften the contrast of a complementary blue and orange scheme in this lively kitchen.

complementary
schemes

Complementary schemes are based on a pair of colors that lie opposite each other on the color wheel. Blue-green and red-orange are complements, as are turquoise and terra-cotta.

A complementary scheme is rich and exciting because the colors visually intensify each other. This is a high-contrast scheme; you can tone it down by pairing intermediate colors, such as blue-violet and yellow-orange, rather than primaries or secondaries such as blue and orange. Using quieter values will also temper a complementary scheme. If no complementary colors appeal to you, you can also create interesting harmony with color pairs that are only approximately opposite, such as yellow-orange and blue or sage green (a yellow-green) and violet.

Blue and yellow-orange prove that approximate opposites can be successful pairs.

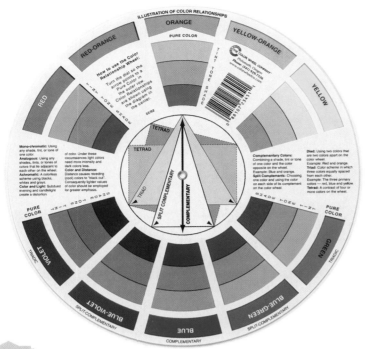

LOWE'S QUICK TIP

Complex schemes can look unbalanced if all the colors are in equal amounts. Make one color dominant and use the others in supporting roles.

Above: The back of the Color Wheel tool (see page 12) helps you identify the components of complex color schemes.

Below: Since blue, red, and yellow are evenly spaced around the color wheel, they form a triad color scheme.

Color Matches **Walls:** Earth Elements Heatwave; column on right: base coat: Valspar Whimsical; glaze: Decorative Effects Slate Blue

complex schemes

Complex schemes consist of more than two colors that are neither complementary nor analogous. If properly chosen, such schemes are pleasing because they automatically balance the visual temperature. Typically, a complex scheme works best in a home with details such as wood mouldings, exposed beams, or columns that can be accented with the supporting colors.

For three-color combinations, you can work successfully with either a "triad" or "split complement." A triad pulls together three colors that are spaced evenly around the color wheel. Consider the richness of golden walls and wine red upholstery with accents in cobalt blue. A split complement, on the other hand, starts with a primary or intermediate color and adds the colors that flank its complementary. In such a scheme, golden walls could be enlivened instead with periwinkle (blue-violet) and magenta (red-violet).

To produce a four-color combination that's even more dynamic, try a "double split complement." This consists of two complementary pairs of colors that are separated from each other by only one position on the color wheel, such as orange and yellow with blue and violet. Or create a "tetrad"—a four-color combination of colors equidistant on the color wheel, like green, yellow-orange, red, and blue-violet.

When working with complex color combinations, don't forget that all the elements in a room, including wood, tile, metal, and fabrics, contribute color and are part of the overall scheme. For example, fir trim (with orange-yellow tones) could be paired with terra-cotta walls (red-orange) and metal light sconces (gray blue) in a triadic scheme.

white, black, and gray

White, black, and shades of gray create a high-contrast scheme that is popular in modern design. Whether used alone or together, these non-colors can be extremely sophisticated, but they can also seem stark in the absence of color.

White is well known for creating a light and airy look. Walls painted white reflect both natural and artificial light; white ceilings reflect 10 percent more light than even the palest hue. Black is graphic and sophisticated. With the exception of the classic black leather sofa or baby grand piano, it should be used in small doses, as an accent to punctuate a design. Paint the drawers in a white cabinet black, for example, or install a black and white tile floor.

A true black and white scheme needs a variety of texture and pattern to provide visual interest. Enliven an all-white room with a black and white striped table or a white and gray textured rug. Soften white or gray walls with a stenciled border in a contrasting neutral. Or, if the look is too austere, add a touch of color—a painting or brightly painted trim. Just as neutrals can calm a colorful scheme, color can enliven a black, white, or gray one.

Top: Touches of red and yellow add hot color to a gray, black, and white scheme.

Right: A one-color scheme is enlivened with shiny metal, glass, and green foliage, all of it subordinate to a panoramic cityscape.

Color Matches **Walls: Earth Elements Standing Rock; trim: American Tradition Ultra White**

Color Match **Walls and trim: Valspar Moon Mist**

aspects of color

DETERMINING WHICH COLORS YOU LIKE AND WHICH ONES YOU WANT TO AVOID is the biggest challenge in the color selection process. However, it is not your only challenge. Once you've decided on a certain color family (for example, blue-greens or red-oranges), move on to the questions of what proportion of each color to use, where to use it, and how to balance value and intensity to create the most harmonious environment. The following pages explore additional aspects of color that will help you make those choices.

color and space

Playing with color allows you to make a room appear smaller, larger, taller, shorter, cozier, or more formal. Visual temperature, value, and intensity all play a role in altering the sense of space in a room. (See pages 108–115 for projects that use color to deal with specific spatial situations.)

The warm colors appear to come closer, so they can be used to make a cavernous room appear smaller or a small room feel intimate and enveloping. Cool colors give the illusion of being farther away. If you want to visually enlarge a room or heighten a ceiling, use cool colors.

You can also play with intensities and values of color to change the apparent proportions of a room. Painting walls a darker color or a more intense one, whether warm or cool, will diminish the size of a room. Similarly, walls painted a lighter or less intense color will make a room feel more open and airy. And finally, contrast also plays a part in altering space. A great deal of contrast will have the same impact as a dark color, reducing the perceived space. Monochromatic and analogous schemes open it up.

This information can help you decide where colors will be most effective in a room. Imagine a color scheme of coral (a light-value, warm color) and teal (an intense, cool color). You have the option of having coral walls and teal trim, which would make the room feel warm and cozy, or teal walls and coral trim, which would create a fresh but cooler atmosphere. Although the same two hues are used, the effects on the room will be dramatically different. Color placement has everything to do with the visual impact of your scheme.

Color can affect our sense of the space in adjoining rooms as well. Carrying the same paint color and flooring from room to room makes for a smooth visual transition and opens up a small home. If you use

A blue-violet nook appears much deeper than the claret red one, although their depths are identical. Red comes forward, while blue recedes.

Color Matches (American Tradition colors) Wall: Woodlawn Whitewash; left nook: Elderberry; right nook: Oatlands Violet

different colors in each room, you create distinctly separate spaces, which might be effective in a large and rambling home. Even when you do this, however, use colors of a similar intensity. The rooms will look different, yet unified.

Right: Warm colors invite you into this cozy living room. The sage green paint on the ceiling adds to the sense of intimacy; its metallic sheen reflects light, preventing a closed-in feeling.

Below: Dark blue walls and trim put the focus on this living room's bright furniture. Lighter blue raises the apparent height of the ceiling.

Color Matches Near room: American Tradition Autumn Morn; far room walls: American Tradition Southern Brick; far room ceiling: base coat: Valspar Olive Hint; glaze: Decorative Effects Metal and Patina Bronze

Color Matches (American Tradition colors)
Walls: New Indigo; ceiling: Filoli Garden Pool

Below: Using red in a living room should keep the conversation lively. The deep blue fireplace surround matches the custom tiles.

Bottom: A red bedroom can help slow starters get moving quickly in the morning. The wall color is Laura Ashley Home's Summer Pudding.

altering mood
with color

Just as color can alter the sense of space, it can also alter the mood of a room. When selecting color, consider how the room will be used. Is the space used for work, play, reading, napping, or entertaining? Is it a personal, family, or public area? More important, how do you want people to feel in these areas? Relaxed, animated, or somewhere in between?

Balancing intensity and tone is one way to affect mood. Any low-contrast scheme is going to be calmer and easier to live with. High-contrast schemes are visually exciting and can overstimulate the senses. Unless you want to create a lot of energy, make one hue dominant, using different amounts of contrasting colors to eliminate tension.

color profiles

Research shows that each color imparts its own unique psychological effect. By knowing how the mind and body may respond to specific colors, you have a better chance of creating rooms that not only look good, but feel right.

RED. Red is an emotionally intense color that increases heart rate and body temperature. It is associated with energy, power, danger, and passion—and it's a color that always commands attention. In studies it has been found to stimulate appetite, making it a good option for dining rooms. Tones of red, such as pink or burgundy, are much easier on the eyes and body than bright red, which is highly stimulating.

Color Matches Upper wall: American Tradition Retro Rust; lower wall and trim: American Tradition Star Lily; fireplace surround: Decorative Effects Translucent Glaze Slate Blue

ORANGE. Less aggressive than red, orange still gives the sensation of warmth and creates a sense of joy. Because it increases oxygen supply to the brain, it enhances mental activity. In its many variations, orange provides an invigorating and welcoming atmosphere.

Below: A neutral rug and pale green bureau moderate the intensity of the bright orange walls in a high-energy room for a child.

Right: A warm orange is inviting in a powder room. This sometimes challenging space is a perfect place to play with vibrant color.

Color Match **Walls: American Tradition Firebush**

Color Matches **(Earth Elements colors)**
Walls: Wildfire; bureau: Tumbleweed

Color Matches **Main wall: Laura Ashley Home Imperial Yellow; left wall and trim: American Tradition Ultra White**

Above: **Painted a vivid yellow, the wall contrasts with adjacent white surfaces to magnify the room's sunlit quality.**

Below: **Always clean and refreshing, aqua reflects the calming influence of blue. Lowe's Earth Elements Fountain of Youth is the lighter hue, paired with Old Man River.**

YELLOW. Yellow, the color of the sun, is an energetic color that can lift the spirits and warm a room. It can also enhance concentration and speed metabolism. While it's associated with happiness, yellow is also disturbing when overused. Studies have shown that people lose their tempers and babies cry more often in yellow rooms.

BLUE. Considered the most relaxing color in the spectrum, blue causes the body to release tension. But it can also create a sense of formality and be cold or even depressing. Blue has been found to be an appetite suppressant, so it should be used only as an accent in areas where you prepare or serve food.

Opposite: **A range of blues creates a tranquil bedroom, highlighted by white furniture and trim. The walls are painted with Olympic's Alaskan Blue; the trim is Olympic's Powderfresh.**

Left: Olympic's Dill, a dark yellow-green, is fresh and sophisticated in a formal living room.

Below: Sage green is an appropriate color for the back-to-nature Arts and Crafts style.

GREEN. The easiest color on the eye, green is both calming and refreshing, providing a feeling of renewal and harmony. It has also been associated with feelings of safety. It is more versatile than blue because it is a blend of warm and cool colors (yellow and blue). One of the basic hues of nature, green is effective in almost any room, but particularly appropriate in kitchens and dining rooms.

VIOLET. Like green, violet (opposite) mixes warm and cool colors. It combines the calming effect of blue with the energy of red. Violet is associated with royalty and luxury, but—perhaps because it is rare in nature—it can feel artificial. It is the favorite color of many young children.

Color Matches (Eddie Bauer Home colors) Walls: Grove; trim: Sunwash

Color Matches Wall: Laura Ashley Home Sapphire 4; door frame: American Tradition Town Hall Blue

WHITE. Although white is a non-color, it does impart a specific mood of cleanliness, purity, and innocence. White reflects all light and is a good choice for rooms with odd or irregular features, because minor flaws will nearly disappear in the absence of color. For anyone who finds imperfections stressful, this can have a direct effect on mood.

Left: Blue-violet, accented here with a touch of its complement, yellow-orange, sets a rich tone for a sitting area.

Below: Painting walls and trim white helps meld traditional architectural details with clean-lined contemporary built-ins.

Color Match Walls and trim: American Tradition White Peony

Color Matches (American Tradition colors)
Walls: Retro Rust; cabinets: Organic Green

high-energy rooms

"High-energy" rooms encourage activity and interaction. One surefire way to create such a room is to cover the walls in a warm and intense color. If you favor the cooler colors, create a dynamic atmosphere by working with bold complementaries or colors in starkly different values or intensities. For instance, add a bright yellow cabinet with red handles to a room with blue walls; what was a cool design will become a lively scheme.

Reds will get the conversation going in a dining or living room, but may be too hot for a kitchen, where the stove already heats things up. Red-oranges are more stimulating than yellow-oranges, which are a little more informal—you could use red-orange in a home office to encourage creativity, and yellow-orange in a great room where family and friends gather. Yellow creates instant warmth as well as energy. Since it can promote concentration, you may want to use it on a single wall behind a desk in a child's bedroom. In its lighter tints, yellow is also a great color to wake up to, helping you start the day right.

Above: Using the complementary colors red and green in lower intensities keeps this kitchen from overheating.

Color Matches (American Tradition colors)
Walls: Del Coronado Amber; trim: Antique White

Above: Bold yellow walls demand equally intense color companions, such as the red and red-orange in the painting and rug.

Right: Lowe's Nickelodeon Colors energize an imaginative kid's room.

places to relax

When you enter your bedroom or private sitting room to read, sleep, or even quietly meditate, you want to feel your whole body slow down and relax. Low-intensity, cool colors will make a room feel open and serene. The most relaxing schemes are monochromatic or analogous (see pages 16–18), but if you use a complex scheme, try similar values or intensities to link different colors and keep the contrast low. Varying the quantities of color also keeps the atmosphere tranquil.

The key to working with cool colors is to add just a hint of warmth. In a pale blue room, paint trim a warm off-white or cover pillows in coral or gold. If you choose an all-blue scheme, be aware that it can seem chilly and unwelcoming. Blue-green or blue-violet are less moody colors that still impart a sense of calm.

Below: Neutrals are always calming, whether they have a warm or cool color in their base.

Right: Yellow towels and flowers provide the touch of warmth a blue bathroom needs.

Color Matches **Walls: Alexander Julian At Home Silverado Trail; trim: American Tradition White**

Color Matches **(American Tradition colors) Walls: Husk Gold; trim and ceiling: White**

31

our perception of color

THE SAME COLORS CAN VARY FROM HOUSE TO HOUSE, AND ROOM TO ROOM, due to factors such as light, contrast, finish, and texture. You'll need to consider all of these as you fine-tune the exact tone, tint, or intensity of the colors you have chosen for your palette. Unfortunately, even if you understand how a color should react under specific conditions, you can't always anticipate exactly how it will look as paint on your wall until you test it. If possible, do a brush-out before beginning any paint job (see page 78).

Color Matches (American Tradition colors)
Walls: Helios Yellow; trim: White

Bright yellow is enhanced by natural sunlight, creating a cheerful dining area for daytime meals.

color and **light**

One factor in how the colors in your home appear to you is each room's exposure to sunlight, which changes with the time of day and the season. North-facing rooms receive less direct sunlight year-round, and that light tends to be cool, making the color in the room darker and duller. South-facing rooms get more and warmer light, which can make colors look brighter and lighter. The conventional wisdom is to balance the color temperature in a room by using warm colors in north-facing rooms and cool colors in south-facing ones. But you can also enhance the color temperature in a room by using colors that match the light's characteristics.

Most light in your home is artificial, and the color of that light varies, too. Warm light from standard incandescent bulbs intensifies yellows, reds, and browns, but tends to dull the cooler colors. Halogen bulbs, a special category of incandescent, produce a white, bright light similar to sunlight. They are effective for highlighting artwork, since they render truer, more natural color. The cool blue light of standard fluorescent bulbs amplifies greens and blues, but muddies warm yellows and reds. Newer fluorescents come closer to providing the warmth of incandescents. Light fixtures can also contribute color to a room. Pendant lights with brightly colored glass shades color the light they give off. A warm-hued lamp shade casts a glow that influences other colors.

The amount of light—whether natural or artificial—also alters value and intensity. Low light darkens value and reduces intensity; a higher light level lightens value and increases intensity.

contrast

Any color can change dramatically because of the colors it is placed next to. For example, yellow on a black background seems to have a darker value than the same yellow on a white background. In general, if the surround is darker, a color appears lighter; if the surround is lighter, the color appears darker.

Two adjacent complementary colors will also enhance or intensify each other. Colors that are not complements may take on some characteristics of the adjacent color. Blue next to red may take on a bit of a violet cast, for example, since blue and red make violet.

Below: Yellow-green and royal blue stripes of equal intensity contrast to brilliant effect in this crisp bedroom.

Right: White trim and accessories emphasize the richness of color on a burgundy colorwashed wall.

Color Matches Walls: base coat: Valspar Rose Bisque; glazes: Decorative Effects Translucent Glaze Maroon and Burnt Sienna; trim: American Tradition Seltzer Water

Color Matches (American Tradition colors) Back wall: Verona Gold and Cobalt Stone; side wall: Oatlands Yellow

Right: A plain wood floor takes on visual texture with a combed pattern in black paint over a brown base coat (see pages 162–163 for instructions on combing).

Opposite: Layers of metallic glaze ragged (see page 159) on the lower wall create visual texture, while torn paper on the upper wall supplies actual texture.

Below: The textured wall of this bathroom was created by dragging Valspar's Decorative Effects Buff glaze over a base coat of Surrey Green. (See pages 150–151 for instructions on dragging.)

Color Matches (American Tradition colors) Floor: base coat: Lyndhurst Mahogany; top coat: Raven Black

texture and finish

There are two types of texture, actual and visual. "Actual" texture is something you can feel, such as grout lines in a tile floor or a grasscloth wall covering. "Visual" texture refers to patterns that appear to the eye as texture, such as faux wood grain or combed lines. Such patterns imply light and shadow, creating the illusion of dimension.

Actual texture modulates color in powerful ways. Its miniscule peaks and valleys absorb rather than reflect light, lowering the intensity of any color. Smooth, shiny surfaces, because they have no real texture, reflect light best and enhance a color's intensity. Texture also affects value. The same color on a shiny surface appears lighter than it does in a textured material. In the exact same color of yellow, a silk pillow will look lighter than a corduroy chair.

When it comes to paint, you can use texture to accentuate the positive or to hide blemishes. High-gloss paint makes architectural features such as mouldings stand out dramatically, but it draws attention to defects like cracks or bumps. The slight texture of a matte finish absorbs light, helping to mask any imperfections.

Combining textures is a balancing act. Too little texture gives a room a flat, dull appearance, but too much is visually confusing. In a neutral or monochromatic scheme, be sure to combine several different textures for visual interest. Match a textured wall, for example, with a smooth leather sofa topped with a pebbly knit throw. When you're working with a more complex color scheme, unite it by using similar textures, such as a shiny wood table and shimmery silk seat cushions, or a sisal rug and chenille-covered sofa. The effects of texture make it nearly impossible to match colors in different materials, such as paint, carpet, and fabric, but the subtle color differences that will result will be interesting.

Color Matches Below chair rail: base coat: Valspar Olive Hint; glaze: Decorative Effects Metal and Patina Bronze; trim: American Tradition Ultra White

pattern

PATTERN UNIFIES COLORS AND TEXTURES WITH DESIGN, BRINGING NEW VITALITY and rhythm to a room. While it may feel safe to limit pattern to fabrics in the room, you can establish the style and personality of a room with pattern on your walls. Stripes, faux wood or stone, checks, plaids, and stenciled designs can all be created with a brush and paint. (Pattern painting projects are presented in the last three chapters.) The key to using painted patterns successfully is to know how patterns will appear on walls and how they will interact.

Wallpaper can also set a theme or provide a supportive background for other design features in a room. Today, the variety of wall coverings is enormous, from playful borders and linen look-alikes to embossed wall coverings designed to look like stucco, pressed tin, or plaster fresco. Most of the textured wall coverings carried at Lowe's can be painted to complement your color scheme. Consult a Lowe's Wall Covering Sales Specialist for advice on choosing and installing the right covering for your walls.

Color Matches (American Tradition colors) Floor: Gypsy Moth; rug: Cortland Buff; shoes: Kettle Black, La Fonda Antique Red (bows), Gypsy Moth (inside)

Above: A sponged-on rug and pair of stylish stenciled high heels bring pattern to a dressing room floor. (See pages 155–156 and 118–125 for instructions on these techniques.)

Opposite: Blue and silver stamped leaves drift randomly across a wall covered in Venetian plaster. (See pages 126–129 and 166–167 for stamping and Venetian plaster projects.)

pattern scale

The size of a design motif or repeated line in a pattern is known as scale. Scale can be small, medium, or large. Small-scale patterns have the softest effect, since they tend to read as textured or solid from a distance. Use them with solids, or as visual relief among other patterns. Medium-scale patterns are more versatile because they retain their design even from a distance, yet rarely overpower other patterns. You can easily use them with small- and large-scale patterns. Use large-scale patterns with care, since large, bold patterns look even bolder over large areas. They can create an atmosphere of grandeur in a large room, but in a small room large-scale patterns have the effect of drawing the walls closer and consuming space.

pattern style

The patterns you may use to decorate your home range from realistic depictions of nature—most commonly flowers, leaves, and wood or stone—to abstracts and geometrics such as stripes, dots, and plaids. The lines in a room will suggest how to

Color Matches (Decorative Effects products) Base: Venetian Plaster Brezza Marino; stamps: Translucent Color Glaze Bluebell and Metal and Patina Glaze Silver

Color Matches **Base coat and trim: American Tradition White Peony; glaze: Decorative Effects Translucent Glaze Slate Blue**

choose and apply pattern. In a room with a high ceiling, avoid strong vertical patterns; instead, try a random pattern or one with a horizontal design. Vertical stripes can raise the ceiling in a low-ceilinged room. In an angular room, patterns that have dominant motifs will be broken as they go in and out of corners. A better choice to unify walls is a small-scale design with no noticeable repeats.

combining patterns

Once you have determined a pattern for the walls, you can combine very different patterns within the room successfully, as long as they share a common color and you don't overdo the mix. Try different patterns on curtains, flooring (including carpets), and furniture. Naturalistic patterns such as florals often combine well with stripes and dots. You can also select similar types of patterns, but use them in different scales, such as small checks with medium-scale plaids. Don't vary the scale too much, though. An oversized pattern and a miniprint may look incompatible together.

When combining different patterns, distribute them throughout the room for a pleasing visual rhythm, and try to create places for the eye to rest by including solid colors or subtly textured materials among them. Clustering patterned materials in one area can make a room look lopsided.

Squares on the wall combine well with the intricacies of the window. The checkerboard pattern and faux wall panels were created by applying a blue glaze over a white base coat. See pages 174–176 for instructions on grid-based patterns such as checkerboards.

Color Matches **(American Tradition colors) Darker diamond: Lexington Green; lighter diamond: Montpelier Olive**

A subtle diamond pattern makes an attractive background for paintings on the wall.

Color Matches (Earth Elements colors) Wall, dark stripe: Dust Storm; light stripe: Whirlwind

Color Matches Plain panel and base coat on right panel: American Tradition Summer Estate; glaze on right panel: Decorative Effects Tintable Glaze in Summer Estate

Above: Stripes, florals, and toiles illustrate a principle of pattern mixing: Repeat colors, while varying the style and scale of the pattern.

Left: In a deft combination, a strié (streaked) pattern dragged horizontally onto the right-hand panel duplicates the background of the figured fabric on the left-hand wall.

LOWE'S QUICK TIP

Always evaluate a pattern from across the room. From a distance, your eye will mix the colors in the pattern—and may create a color you don't like.

color in your home

ARMED WITH A BASIC UNDERSTANDING OF COLOR THEORY, you're ready to consider more specific color palettes for your home. The best place to start is with the colors that appeal to you. But how do you know which ones will be most effective? How will they work with existing furnishings? Where do you turn for inspiration? If you're feeling overwhelmed, relax. At this stage of the hunt, you are collecting ideas, not making final decisions. Your personal palette will naturally develop as you collect samples and consider the possibilities. This chapter presents guidelines to make the search productive and to help you determine how to use color to its best effect.

There are many great sources for color ideas, including the paint department at Lowe's, design magazines, design showcases, fabrics, friends' homes, and natural materials such as flowers, trees, and stones. These are all good starting points. But there is more to living with a color than just liking it. What might be your favorite color for clothing or furniture may not be so appealing when it's brushed across your walls. Popular colors that work in a design magazine may clash with artwork you want to highlight or be unsuitable for the architectural style of your home.

Using the guidelines in this chapter, gather as many different color combinations as you can, putting aside any preconceived notions of what will and won't work. Then, be flexible when assigning the color treatments you like to the rooms in your home.

practical considerations

TAKE A GOOD LOOK AT THE ROOM OR ROOMS YOU'RE GOING TO REDECORATE. Where are your opportunities to use color? The walls and floor are the most obvious places, and changes there will have the greatest visual impact. Furnishings, both soft and hard, are another option. If you like the wall color, but think the room lacks style, paint a table or chairs a bold color or create a striking painted canvas rug. (See "Simple Paint Projects," pages 103–137, for quick projects and "Decorative Effects for Furnishings and Woodwork," pages 179–217, for other projects that add color to furnishings.) Alternatively, use paint to play up interesting architectural details.

If you plan to paint the walls, look carefully for all the factors that will affect your color choices for the room. "All About Color," pages 9–39, touches on some of these, such as the colors of adjacent rooms (see pages 22–23) and variations in natural and artificial light (see pages 32–33). But there are many other issues to consider, including your planned use of the space, focal points in the room, and existing elements that you don't plan to change. These factors can help you determine the best values and intensities of your chosen colors, as well as how much of each to use, and where.

Right: Add a distinctive touch to a child's room with painted furniture. Here a slender chest of drawers and wastebasket are striped to match the cushion (see pages 112–113 for striping instructions).

Below: A vibrant floor mat—acrylic paint applied to the underside of a linoleum remnant and varnished—spices up a monochrome color scheme.

Color Matches Left wall: Waverly Home Classics Burnt Orange; door and trim: American Tradition Swiss Coffee; furniture: (American Tradition colors) Forest Bog and Swiss Coffee

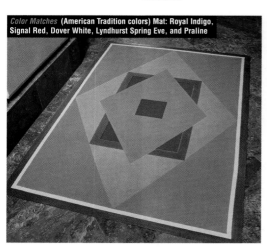

Color Matches (American Tradition colors) Mat: Royal Indigo, Signal Red, Dover White, Lyndhurst Spring Eve, and Praline

function

A room's function is one of the best guides for color selection. A living room is often more decorative than less formal rooms. A child's room can handle bold colors, whereas adults prefer quieter, more contemplative bedrooms.

If you are the only one using the space, you can rely on your own color preferences. A room also used by other family members calls for colors that will meet with their approval—and match their personalities as well as your own.

High-intensity primary and secondary colors energize an informal kitchen. The chairs, painted in different colors, are lively accents to the bright red walls.

Color Matches (American Tradition colors) Wall: Red Decadence; chairs: Red Decadence, Blue Ridge Mountain, and Dark Ivy

Color Matches Wall: American Tradition White and Nickelodeon colors Pawprint Blue, Troll Gold, and Rip Curl Red; cabinets (American Tradition colors): Polo Green (background), Emerald Green, and White; floor (American Tradition colors): White, Woodrow Wilson Putty, Lyndhurst Timber, Ancient Land, and Pipe Smoke

While this bright and energetic landscape would be busy in a master bedroom, it creates a perfect fantasy world for a child. The faux-stone floor completes the outdoor theme.

Color Matches (American Tradition colors)
Walls: Forest Shadow; trim: Chalk

Color Matches (American Tradition colors) Archway:
La Fonda Ortiz Gold; checkerboard: light squares,
Autumn Morn; dark squares, Spiced Orange

focal points

Make sure your room has a main focal point. A room with no emphasis looks monotonous, and one with too many emphasized elements feels chaotic. If you have a major piece of art, an antique rug, a fireplace, or a bay window with a garden view, you may want to build your color scheme around it. Once you've identified the focus, choose colors that make other elements such as walls and floors subordinate, providing a noncompetitive background. Between the focal point and the background areas, look for secondary elements of interest to create a good sense of balance.

existing colors, textures, and patterns

Any new colors you introduce to a room must coordinate with the colors that are already there. When you put together a color scheme, it's easy to forget that all surfaces have color. The wood in floors, paneling, and furniture can vary in hue from dark reds and pink-grays to orange-yellows and dark browns. Even surfaces painted white have a slight tone of color—a creamy yellow, a touch of green or blue, or a hint of red. Metal has color, too, and even most glass has color.

The same applies to textures and patterns. An oak floor puts a wood-grain pattern into the mix, not just a red- or yellow-brown color. A floral sofa adds color and pattern, too. Ornate moulding creates a surface that could be highlighted.

Above: A dark green wall recedes into the background, assuring that the spotlighted painting is the center of attention.

Left: The checkered pattern on the wall—orange-yellow squares painted over straw-yellow—takes its cue from the yellow tones and border of the hardwood floor.

design considerations

ONCE YOU'VE TAKEN STOCK OF THE PRACTICAL CONSIDERATIONS FOR A ROOM, it's time to put your creative side to work, finding ways to balance color, texture, and pattern in the most harmonious way. Happily, there are proven techniques that eliminate guesswork and provide a range of options to suit any taste.

color **balance**

There are several ways to create balance in a color scheme that will influence your color choices. The most harmonious designs use colors in unequal quantities, with one dominant color and one or more supporting ones. As long as the quantities of color vary, this treatment allows you to put together intense hues from around the color wheel. While it is a good rule of thumb to use similar values or intensities in multicolor schemes, too much sameness can lead to boredom. Tend toward low-intensity colors for walls, floors, and large furnishings, and use more intense ones as accents on trim, pillows, or other accessories.

You can use colors in equal quantities if their values and intensities are similar. See page 109 for advice on using paired colors on adjacent or opposing walls; the same tactic can be used with colors on walls and a floor.

LOWE'S QUICK TIP

Consider adding color and texture to stairways or halls, where you won't have to coordinate with furnishings. Often color at the end of a hallway adds a sense of focus to the space.

Color Matches (American Tradition colors) Left wall, above: Pepper Red; right wall: Violet Etiquette; trim and left wall, below: White

Color Matches (Laura Ashley Home colors) Walls: dark stripe, Cowslip 4; light stripe, Cowslip 2

Left: A four-color combination—the red-orange and violet walls, the yellow-toned wood, and the blue-green chairs—is in balance because the value of all colors is similar.

Above: Subtle stripes of low-intensity yellow on the walls balance accents of vibrant color throughout this playful bedroom.

contrasting **trim**

Most homes have some form of trim, which can be either highlighted or downplayed with color. If you wish, trim colors can also visually alter a room's dimensions. A low ceiling will appear higher if you emphasize the verticality of doors and narrow windows with strong color on the casings, and a light-colored high ceiling seems lower if it includes dark beams. In large rooms, small doors or windows seem bigger if the trim is large and has been painted a different color than the walls. When horizontal trim, such as chair rail or picture rail, contrasts with the wall color, a room seems wider or shorter than it really is.

LOWE'S QUICK TIP

If you paint rooms in different colors, use a common color for all trim as well as for transition areas, such as hallways and entries, to tie individual spaces together.

Color Matches **(American Tradition colors) Walls: Full Moon; frieze: La Fonda Ortiz Gold; ceiling, fireplace surround, and trim: Woodlawn Whitewash**

White moulding on the ceiling and wall defines the frieze of darker color, helping lower the ceiling and broaden a narrow seating area.

Color Matches Wall, above: mixture of Earth Elements colors Tawny Bluff, Wildwood, and Burnished Copper; below: base coat: Valspar Macadamia; glazes: Decorative Effects Translucent Glazes Mocha and Burnt Sienna

This scheme relies on texture and pattern to add visual depth and interest to a sitting room. The two different techniques—ragging above and combing below—join with different colors to define upper and lower sections on the wall.

Color Matches Base coat: Decorative Effects Venetian Plaster Amethyst; glaze: Decorative Effects Translucent Opal Glaze, Golden Opal Gloss

Musical notes stenciled in an iridescent glaze over light coral Venetian plaster make a subtle pattern, visible only in reflected light.

special paint effects

Using a decorative paint technique adds texture, pattern, and visual depth to your color scheme. It also provides a more personal, creative touch to a room that solid color can't achieve. Decorative painting ranges from the application of one or more layers of translucent glaze over a base color to antique finishes that make your walls look wonderfully aged. It includes applied details such as stripes, stencils, and stamps, and faux surfaces such as wood or stone. Such techniques provide texture and pattern to suit different styles. See the last three chapters for a variety of decorative painting projects for walls, floors, furnishings, and woodwork.

inspiration

WHERE DO YOU TURN FOR INSPIRATION WHEN YOU DON'T HAVE A CLUE WHAT colors to use in your home? If you look around your environment, you'll find no shortage of ideas to guide you, from the natural world, to colorful items you love, to specific architectural styles. Gather every possibility that strikes your fancy, then decide what single colors or combinations are most appealing and effective.

If you end up with too many different colors to choose from, or can't visualize a combination you like using the materials you've collected, Lowe's can help you create color schemes that match your preferences. See page 79 for a review of our color selection services and programs.

Color Matches **Left wall: American Tradition Neptune's Sea; right wall: Earth Elements Driftwood**

colors in **nature**

If the atmosphere you are seeking is fresh and natural, turn to the garden for inspiration. Take your color cues from your own plantings, or collect photos of other gardens you love. You'll soon notice a pattern to your choices—perhaps a preference for the various shades of green in a shade garden or the soft pastels of a romantic rose border. You might be drawn to the bright colors of a bed full of dahlias or a field of sunflowers. As you begin to narrow down the shades you prefer, gather paint chips, or even flower cuttings, and use them to project how those colors work together. Don't overlook subtle earth tones; note how they accent the colors of the garden. Consider the brown of the tree trunks, the gray of a stone wall, or the dark red of a brick pathway.

A garden outside the window inspires this corner, where a blue-green wall pairs with an olive green one, and fruits and foliage are featured in the painting, lamp, and table design.

Decorative painting carries out a drawn-from-nature theme on this colorful chest, which showcases green faux-marbling on the top and hand-painted vines over a golden glaze on its sides.

Color Matches **Base coat: Decorative Effects Translucent Glaze Maize; decoration: American Tradition colors Great Barrington and La Fonda Sante Fe Brown**

a **favorite** object

A piece of fabric, a special rug, a painting, or a china pattern may provide a comfortable starting point for developing a color scheme. The object should be one you love and it should contain more—rather than fewer—colors. The advantage of a multicolored object is that it provides a ready-made palette. But don't think you have to use all of its colors; pick out those you like the best. Because texture or pattern can affect color, don't try to make exact matches. Instead, seek out colors for your scheme that blend well together. If the item you are starting with has a red-violet, for instance, find a warmer red that blends well with it.

To find compatible colors, also look at the item from a distance. You may discover some overall colors that escape the eye close up. A green fabric with a yellow design, for example, may seem to be olive when you stand back. Try introducing this perceived color, even though it doesn't actually exist in your favorite object.

Color Matches Wall: Earth Elements Firefly; trim: American Tradition White

Orange-yellow walls are perfectly matched to the dominant color in a collection of hand-painted plates. Lowe's can color-match paint to any item.

Color Matches (American Tradition colors) Wall: White; stencils: Landscape, East Side Gold, Cliveden Colonial Rose, and Maiden's Blush

The main color in this stenciled floral pattern is drawn from a favorite chair. The artist hand-painted additional colors and details over the stencil—a trick anyone can use to individualize a precut stencil.

For a neoclassical home, a warm beige is appropriate, as is the faux-marble treatment on the columns, pilasters, wainscot, and mouldings.

architectural style

The architectural style of your home—or the style you'd like to suggest—provides plenty of inspiration for color selection.

Until about two hundred years ago, only sixteen pigments were used in paint. Therefore, for a home in an older style, there's a fairly narrow set of "authentic" choices. Several paint companies—such as Valspar with its American Tradition paints, available at Lowe's—have color palettes appropriate to period styles, which can make your job even easier. However, while sticking with architectural guidelines is helpful, especially if you have an authentic period house, remember that there are many other sources of inspiration that can be just as effective.

traditional

Homes built between 1607 and 1850 in the United States are often referred to as traditional in style. But your house doesn't have to be that old to take on a traditional look. Just make sure that its overall appearance and character suit this style.

Homes in the Colonial style (1607–1780) were followed by the more imposing Georgian (1740–1790) and Federal (1790–1850) styles, each of which borrowed ideas from its predecessors. Colonial architecture is a collection of regional styles from the thirteen colonies. Georgian and Federal are neoclassical, reinterpreting Greek and Roman design elements.

A Colonial home looks most authentic if you use earth tones, including yellow, almond, red, and brown, as well as both bright and lighter values of blue, green, and yellow. White or almond walls with painted trim are typical of the period, but you can also use color on your walls and paint your trim white. For the more formal Georgian style, use cream, pea green, deep pink, or pastel colors on the walls. Architectural details such as mouldings or columns can be painted white or stone color, or given a faux-marble treatment (see pages 170–173).

Terra-cotta, stone, deep pinks, and grays are the traditional colors of the Federal style. Red is popular for dining rooms, and greens can tie interior rooms to gardens. Consider painting wall paneling to resemble mahogany (see pages 198–201), or try painting baseboards with faux-wood or faux-marble designs. Scenic wallpaper and borders or panels decorated with classical motifs are typical of the Federal style; you can replicate them easily on walls using stencils (see pages 118–125).

victorian

Typified by high ceilings and elaborate mouldings, the Victorian style accommodates a rich color palette, stained wood, and lots of pattern. When the walls are not covered in stained wood, they can be painted in dark shades of red, purple, or green, or the lighter hues of salmon, mauve, blue-green, or lilac. Wallpaper can be used liberally in the Victorian style, with several patterns on the same wall separated by moulding. Wallpaper borders can also be hung above the wainscot on the lower part of a wall, or under the ceiling moulding. Painted trim should be either darker or lighter than the walls, but not the same color. Trim and furniture made of softwood can be painted to resemble hardwood (see pages 198–201).

A contemporary room can take on Victorian style when period details are applied. In this high-ceilinged room, dark color and a wallpaper border help create the period look.

Color Matches **(American Tradition colors) Walls: Old Burgundy; ceiling: Labyrinth; archway and next room: Full Moon**

Color Matches Walls: Eddie Bauer Home Pine Needle; ceiling: American Tradition Antique White

A hallmark of the Arts and Crafts style is woodwork painted in a natural color, such as this pale sage green. The wallpaper border is also typical of the style.

arts and crafts

The Arts and Crafts style, which emerged during the late nineteenth and early twentieth centuries, places an emphasis on craftsmanship and the intrinsic beauty of the building materials themselves. Natural colors like cream, sage green, olive, or earthy red are truest to the Arts and Crafts style. Stained wood trim is very common in homes of this period, but you can also paint the trim a natural color to contrast with white or cream walls. For a simple decorative touch, paint stencils along the top of a wall or on the ceiling between exposed beams. If you prefer to use wallpaper to add pattern to the room, look for simple leaf or floral patterns in two or three natural colors. William Morris and other patterns from the Arts and Crafts era are available.

cottage

Cottage style is an adaptation of the earliest American building traditions. The style is typified by walls covered in white beadboard or tongue-and-groove wainscoting. Walls are often left white, but pastels such as pale yellows, blues, and pinks are good colors for Cottage style. To lend a Cottage atmosphere to a newer home, try distressing or pickling woodwork (see pages 188–191).

Blue walls and floor (Wave from Lowe's Eddie Bauer Home collection) with white paneling (Eddie Bauer Oyster) evoke the casual airiness of a Cottage home.

mediterranean country

The rough plaster walls of French farm-houses and the stone surfaces of Italian villas give depth to the earthy colors typical of these styles. Neutral colors are also popular in both styles, creating a sophisticated decor. You can give an aged patina to the walls of a newer home by colorwashing them with neutral color glazes (see pages 140–144). Create a faux-marble or lime-stone finish for visual interest in a home with Tuscan detailing (see pages 170–173 and 177–179).

latin

The Spanish Colonial and Southwestern styles both draw their color palettes from the land and sky. The rough plaster walls of the Spanish Colonial are often covered in rich terra-cottas, pinks, ochres, and deep blues. Painted borders and outlines around doors and windows are also typical of the style. Southwestern plaster walls are generally smoother and borrow colors from the desert and its vivid sunsets, ranging from the neutral tone of sand to bright aquas, corals, and fuchsias. You can add texture to flat wallboard to create the look of old plaster, as described on pages 166–167. Colorwashing (see pages 140–144) will provide visual texture on a flat surface.

Walls colorwashed in tints of sand look aged, matching the heavy bronze sconces in a Mediterranean-inspired home.

Color Matches Base coat: Valspar Jalapeno; glaze: Decorative Effects Translucent Glaze Moss

Color Matches Walls: Earth Elements Swelter; doors: American Tradition Cobalt Stone; ceiling and border: American Tradition Ultra White

Bold yellow and dark blue provide high contrast in an open Spanish Colonial dining room. Notice how the white border painted around the door mimics trim.

scandinavian folk

The Scandinavian folk style includes lots of wood paneling and simple trims, often with scalloped edges. Painted designs on door and window casings, beams, shelves, and cabinetry give the style its distinctive characteristics. Deep blues and greens are popular background colors for designs in white, red, and yellow. Use stenciling or stamping techniques to apply your own (see pages 118–129).

Color Matches (American Tradition colors) Walls: Harper's Ferry; trim and seats: American Tradition Neptune's Sea; window: Southern Sunrise; additional colors in stencils: White and Bonfire Red

Playful stencils and hand-painted designs across a dark green and blue wall are typical of the Scandinavian folk style.

asian

Both Japanese and Chinese architectural styles have distinctive palettes. In Japanese architecture, the non-colors (black, white, and gray) are stressed. The effect is to fade objects into a neutralized state where shape rather than color dominates. Often, exposed wood is painted black to enhance its silhouette effect. White rice-paper shoji screens bring in light from outside, creating shadows through backlighting. Red, inspired by the sun and fire, is the primary color used to accent the clean lines of the architecture.

In traditional Chinese architecture, the practice of feng shui affects color selection. Feng shui is an ancient Chinese belief system that works with the five Chinese elements of wood, fire, earth, metal, and water to bring energetic balance into a home. There are so many interpretations of the traditional practice that no discussion of color in feng shui can be definitive. But all agree that colors, like the elements, should be kept in balance. Blue (wood), red (fire), yellow (earth), white (metal), and black (water) symbolize the five natural elements, and are important colors in Chinese design.

Venetian plaster walls, finished with a gold metallic wax, create the illusion of rice paper, a fitting backdrop for the high contrast and minimal color of this Asian-influenced setting.

Color Matches Wall and wood under stairs: base coat: Valspar Casba Melon; glazes: Decorative Effects products Translucent Glaze Brilliant Red and Metal and Patina Glaze Copper; wall under stairs: base coat: Valspar Casba Melon; glazes: Decorative Effects Translucent Glazes Buff and Maize

contemporary

When you look at homes being built today, you'll see characteristics borrowed from different eras. Over the past several decades, designers and builders have revived and reinterpreted a number of earlier styles, including elements of traditional, Victorian, Arts and Crafts, and Cottage architecture. Modernism, with its clean lines, absence of decoration, and white walls, still influences many architects. But today's designs often blend classical formal motifs, such as columns and pilasters, with modern-day functions such as the popular kitchen/family room combination, resulting in a more eclectic, casual style. In this almost-anything-goes era, you can borrow color ideas directly from the traditions of the past or develop your own to suit your preferences and lifestyle.

Color Matches **(American Tradition colors) Walls:** Gilded Green; **ceiling:** Pale Shadow; **trim:** Violet Wisp; **window grid:** Rose Blossom; **window trim:** Hen's Egg; **table: top,** Waterbury; **legs,** Caribbean Garden; **shelf,** Winterberry

Top: Exotic painting techniques, such as the gilding and faux lapis used on this stairwell, are used liberally by contemporary designers. Here, the color ideas are borrowed from ancient Egyptian art.

Above: A complex color scheme executed in pastel tints renders a 1950s ranch-house living room contemporary.

Color Match Wall: American Tradition Oatlands Violet

Color Matches Living room walls: Eddie Bauer Home Meadow; kitchen walls: Eddie Bauer Home Daffodil; hallway walls: Eddie Bauer Home Grenadine; trim: American Tradition White

Color Matches Main wall: base coat: Valspar Carolina Denim; glaze: Decorative Effects Translucent Glaze Bluebell; dining room wall: American Tradition Field Green; loft wall: American Tradition Biscuit; trim: American Tradition Canyon Clay

Above left: High-intensity violet walls break with past tradition to provide a warm background for the painting.

Above right: The green leather sofa and dark red and gold cushions provide the inspiration for the multicolor paint scheme here and in the adjoining rooms. White trim ties the rooms together.

Left: A typically Victorian palette of violet, green, and peach is given a modern twist by combining light pastels with high-intensity versions of the colors.

painting tools and techniques

PAINTING IS SOMETHING THAT ANYONE WITH TIME CAN learn to do, and anyone with time and patience can do well. If you're a veteran painter, you may want to skim this chapter, then move on to the last three chapters for ideas on great painting projects you can do yourself. If not, spend some time with this chapter to learn more about the tools and materials you'll need— from classic brushes and paints to the latest innovations—as well as easy ways to prepare for painting, apply the paint, and clean up after almost any interior painting project. The following pages also provide tips and shortcuts to save you time and help avoid mistakes, and important information about using paint safely and disposing of it responsibly.

Once you master these basics, you can tackle anything from painting a wall to creating decorative faux finishes that can turn your home into a showcase (see the last two chapters). Remember, too, that Lowe's Paint Sales Specialists are always available to guide you in your purchases and answer any questions you have about paint and how to apply it (see page 79).

Always wear latex gloves for projects with alkyd paints and finishes to protect your hands from harmful chemicals as well as hard-to-remove color.

Color Matches on photos, designating paints available at Lowe's, have been provided by Valspar. Due to the limitations of the printing process, colors printed on the pages of this (or any) book may not be an exact representation of a specified paint or specialty product. Check paint chips at Lowe's for the true colors. If you like the color on the page better than the one on the paint chip, a Lowe's Paint Sales Specialist can mix a match for you.

all about paint

ALL TYPES OF PAINT PROTECT AND DECORATE THE SURFACES TO WHICH THEY are applied. However, not every paint is of equal quality, or appropriate for every situation. Whether you're rolling paint on a wall or using a decorative technique, a basic understanding of the various types of paint and their formulations will help you select the best product for your project.

varieties of paint

Paint is made up of four basic ingredients: pigments, which provide color; a binder, which holds pigment particles together and adheres them to the surface being painted; additives, which can enhance certain properties such as brushing ease, mildew resistance, drying time, and sheen (see page 62); and a liquid, which acts as a carrier for the other three.

The pigments, binder, and additives are what's left on the surface after the liquid evaporates. In general, paints that contain more of these ingredients in higher qualities will dry to a thicker film, providing better coverage and protection.

The two most common binders are latex and alkyd, both of which are synthetic materials. There are three types of latex binder—acrylic, modified acrylic, and vinyl. All three types are formulated with water as the main liquid ingredient; as a result, latex paint is also known as "water-base." Alkyd binder is mixed with a volatile—that is, evaporating—solvent to form alkyd paint. The solvent used to dissolve the alkyd is mineral spirits (also known as paint thinner). Because earlier paints used natural oils instead of alkyd as the binder, this type of paint is often called "oil-base."

Alkyd paint can be applied over latex paint. However, don't paint over an old alkyd coat with vinyl latex; apply a coat of an alkyd primer or acrylic latex primer before painting.

primer

Primer, which comes in both latex and alkyd formulations, is used as a first coat to seal a porous, absorbent surface and make paint adhere to it better. It is also used to separate coats of incompatible paint, such as alkyd and latex or wood stain and latex. Some primers have stain blockers that seal in stains, ink and crayon marks, grease, and smoke marks. Mildewcide can be added to any primer to reduce the likelihood of mildew stains appearing, or reappearing after they have been cleaned with a mildew remover.

A painted surface in good condition that's compatible with the new paint you have chosen may not need an additional primer. Keep in mind, however, that it is often less expensive and labor-intensive to use a primer and a single coat of paint rather than two—or more—coats of the paint alone. Consult the chart on page 66 to see if you need to use a primer and, if so, what type to use.

latex paint

Latex is the most popular type of paint sold today, and for good reason. Because its liquid base is water, latex paint dries quickly, is practically odorless, poses the least threat to the environment, and cleans up easily with soap and water. (Most latex paint does include a small quantity of volatile solvents as well—see page 62.) One limitation to bear in mind is that it should be applied in temperatures above 50 degrees F. Latex paint is an ideal choice for painting over plaster, wallboard, and wood trim. While even the best latex finishes are more likely to show brush marks than alkyd paint, they do have better gloss (sheen) and color retention and also offer better resistance to chipping.

The quality of a latex paint is affected by the kind of binder used. The highest quality and most durable latex paint contains 100 percent acrylic resin. Known as acrylic latex, this paint offers excellent adhesion even when applied over alkyds. It is the best choice for wood trim. It goes on easily, without spattering, is stain resistant (meaning household dirt and stains don't adhere to it easily), and, if it does get dirty, is able to withstand scrubbing. In "modified" acrylic latex paint, an acrylic binder is modified with styrene. This paint also has good adhesion and stain resistance. It is especially good to use in its semigloss or gloss form (see "Sheen" on page 62) on surfaces that come together under pressure—such as a set of window sashes or a door and its jamb—because it has great block resistance (the quality of not sticking to itself upon contact). Vinyl latex paint, the least expensive, uses a vinyl binder. It offers satisfactory performance as a flat (low-gloss) paint; the semigloss formulation works well in low-traffic areas where dirt is least likely to accumulate.

alkyd paint

Some people prefer to use alkyd paint, especially on woodwork, because it is durable, stain resistant, and dries virtually free of brush marks. It can also be sanded easily. Although it is an improvement on

Color Matches Walls: base coat: Valspar Bronco; glaze: Decorative Effects Translucent Glaze Maroon; ceiling and trim: American Tradition Bone White

Well-chosen paint—the right formulation, sheen, and color—can make almost any redecorating project a success.

the old-fashioned oil paints, alkyd paint still has a stronger smell and more impact on the environment than latex paint (see below). The alkyd binder takes a day or more to oxidize, or cure, so you must allow extra time between coats or before touching the surface. With some brands of alkyd paints, the oxidation continues indefinitely, which can result in yellowing and excessive hardness. Alkyd paint requires paint thinner for cleanup, making it messier to deal with. Alkyd paint is not appropriate for masonry or other alkaline surfaces such as plaster or galvanized metal.

milk paint

Milk paint is a natural product that has been used for centuries. The paint, which is sold as a powder to be mixed with water, is made from milk protein (also called casein), clay, natural pigments, and lime. It can also be diluted with more water to create a natural stain. Milk paint dries quickly to a soft, flat, and almost chalky finish, with a slightly uneven texture, that gives the impression of age. Due to its expense, it is used most often on wood furniture, but it is also a good choice for anyone who wants to avoid chemicals. Milk paint is available at craft and antique stores and over the Internet. See pages 196–197 for more about applying milk paint.

sheen

Both latex and alkyd paint are available in different sheens—light-reflecting qualities—ranging from flat to glossy. Sheen affects both appearance and performance. Manufacturers label finishes differently, but typically there are four categories.

A "flat" or "matte" finish is nonreflective and is the most forgiving finish for surfaces with imperfections. A flat paint is ideal for most walls and ceilings, especially in living rooms and bedrooms that receive less wear. Its rougher texture is difficult to clean, however, so if you use flat or matte paint, you should definitely keep a can of touchup paint on hand.

"Eggshell," "satin," or "low luster" paints are a bit more lustrous in appearance than flat paint, with eggshell having the lowest sheen of the three. These paints are more stain resistant than flat paint and work well in areas prone to dirt, such as hallways, bathrooms, kitchens, and kids' rooms. They also impart warmth to woodwork without being shiny.

"Semigloss" paint has a medium luster that is very stain resistant and easy to clean. It is a popular finish for areas prone to moisture, grease, or heavy wear, such as on the walls and ceilings of bathrooms and kitchens, or on wood doors and trim.

PAINT AND THE ENVIRONMENT

Although paint has come a long way since the old lead-base days, it still contains ingredients that can be harmful both to you and to the environment. Its main environmental problem is that it contains solvents that release volatile organic compounds (VOCs) into the air as they evaporate. VOCs can sometimes take days or weeks to leave the paint film. Paint companies have worked in recent years to reduce the amount of volatile solvents in their products, replacing them with nonvolatile oil or resin.

By its nature, latex paint has fewer volatile solvents than alkyd paint—typically 2 to 8 percent for latex versus 40 to 50 percent for alkyd. You may even be able to find a latex paint with no VOC content. (The downside to zero-VOC latex paint is that it dries so quickly it can be difficult to handle.) Because of toxicity, some natural (non-alkyd) oil-base paint is restricted or illegal in certain areas.

Regardless of which paint you use, always ventilate the area well with open windows and fans. Choose brushing and rolling over spraying to minimize fumes. Dispose of paint properly to avoid environmental hazards. For more about how to safely work with paints, see page 69. For more information on paint cleanup, storage, and disposal, see pages 98–101.

"Gloss" paint, also known as "high-gloss," reflects more light than any other finish and is more eye-catching. High-gloss paint is sometimes referred to as enamel because of its shiny, lacquer finish. While it is the toughest, most durable, and most stain resistant finish, gloss paint will also highlight any imperfections in your walls or wood, so it's especially important to smooth out rough spots and fill and sand all nail holes before you paint. Since gloss paint is the easiest to clean, use it in high-traffic areas that attract fingerprints, dirt, and other abuses. It is an effective and practical choice for kitchen and bathroom walls, banisters and railings, and doorway, window, baseboard, and other interior trim.

Like trim, kitchen cabinetry benefits from semigloss paint, which gives it a sturdy, easy-to-clean surface.

Color Matches Walls: Laura Ashley Home Pale Cowslip 5; cabinets and trim: (American Tradition colors) Red Decadence, Farewell Blue, and Royal Indigo

special products for decorative painting

A crackle finish adds character to these furnishings. See page 137 for a crackle-finish project. On both mirror and table, Decorative Effects Weathered Crackle Glaze covers a base coat of Pale Wheat. The top coat on the mirror is American Tradition La Fonda Antique Red; on the table it's La Fonda Trail Green.

Decorative painting has become much easier since commercially prepared specialty products have become available. When you use these products, read the instructions carefully to make sure you are applying them as intended, with the right primers, base coats, and other paint products. You'll find projects using these paints in the last three chapters.

commercially prepared glazes

Pretinted latex glazes, some with metallic or pearl finishes, take the mess and work out of creating a glaze for most of the decorative painting techniques used today. They can be used wherever a technique calls for a latex or acrylic glaze (sometimes called a wash). Follow the manufacturer's instructions, and test to make sure the consistency is appropriate for the effect you wish to achieve. For more on glazes, see page 70.

crackle glaze

Crackle glaze is a special formulation that is applied between coats of paint, causing the top coat to crack and reveal the base coat. The result is a rustic, naturally weathered finish. Different products work with specific paint types, so be sure to follow the glaze manufacturer's directions in selecting your paint.

metallic glaze

Applied over a base coat of paint, these glazes impart a solid or brushed metal finish to walls or furniture. Metallic glazes come in colors to replicate real metal, including brass, copper, silver, and bronze.

texture paints

Texture paints can be used to add texture to flat walls, creating effects such as brushed suede, grasscloth, or plaster, as well as leather and sand. Most come in a range of colors and can be rolled, brushed, or, in thicker applications, troweled on a wall.

stencil paint

Formulated specifically for stenciling, stencil paint is an acrylic paint premixed with medium (a thinning agent) that is sold in small bottles to avoid waste. The consistency of the paint will vary among brands, so test it before applying it to your surface. If it is too thick, it can be diluted with acrylic medium, which you can purchase at an art supply store.

artist's oils and acrylics

Used to tint oil glazes and to create faux (that is, false or imitation) effects such as wood graining and marbling, artist's oils and acrylics are available in art supply stores. Both come in tubes. Acrylics also come in a liquid form, sold in jars. Colors vary from brand to brand, so if you run out of a color, be sure when you buy more that it's the same brand.

Covering walls with texture, such as this Valspar Brushed Suede finish (the color is Vista), enlivens a sophisticated neutral color scheme. See page 133 for instructions on creating a brushed suede finish.

interior paints **for all surfaces**

SURFACE	FIRST COAT	FINISH COAT	NOTES
NEW WALLBOARD	Prime with latex primer and let dry at least 4 hours	Apply one or two coats of latex or alkyd paint	Don't use alkyd primer—it will raise nap in paper
NEW PLASTER	Prime with latex primer and let dry at least 4 hours	Apply one or two coats of latex or alkyd paint	None
PAINTED WALLBOARD OR PLASTER	If the surface is dirty, wash and rinse thoroughly. Sand existing paint to remove surface imperfections. Dust. If you are applying latex paint over old alkyd paint, apply an acrylic latex primer.	Apply one or two coats of latex or alkyd paint	To test if the existing paint is alkyd or latex, apply denatured alcohol to a small section. Latex will dissolve; alkyd won't.
BARE WOOD	Use an acrylic latex primer or latex enamel primer. Use a stain-blocking primer for wood that stains or leaches severely.	Lightly sand primer to remove brush marks, dust, and apply one or two coats of finish paint	The minimum sheen for woodwork is eggshell
PAINTED WOOD	Remove loose, flaking paint and sand smooth. Dust. Spot-prime any bare wood with acrylic latex or latex enamel primer.	Apply a first coat of latex or alkyd paint; let it dry thoroughly. Sand lightly, then apply a second coat.	The minimum sheen for woodwork is eggshell
MASONRY	Clean the surface well with a stiff bristle or wire brush. For a very porous surface, apply masonry sealer. For a rough surface like cinder block, use latex block filler.	Apply one or two coats of acrylic latex paint	Look for white, powdery residue, a sign of moisture in masonry. If you find it, check the exterior walls for drainage problems and repair as needed.
METAL	Remove rust with a wire brush. Prime metals that contain iron with latex primer or alkyd corrosion-resistant primer. Prime galvanized metal or aluminum with acrylic latex primer. If you are using alkyd paint, prime galvanized metal with corrosion-resistant primer. Apply two coats of primer.	Apply one or two coats of acrylic latex or alkyd paint	Flat finish paint is not recommended

protective finishes

A protective finish is a clear coating that goes over faux finishes or bare or stained woodwork to make them more durable and easier to clean. Most clear coatings are known as varnishes. Oil-base varnishes are the most durable. Newer water-base varnishes are easier to clean up and less harmful to the environment. Like paint, protective finishes come in a range of sheens, from matte to gloss.

Woodwork, floors, and furniture can be finished by anyone, but it is extremely difficult to varnish walls—leave that to a professional.

Protective finishes are often applied to woodwork immediately after staining. To prepare bare wood for a stain followed by a protective finish, sand it smooth, dust it with a tack cloth, and apply the stain. Once the stain is dry, apply one coat of protective finish and let it dry overnight. Sand lightly with steel wool or fine sandpaper. Apply at least three more coats, drying and sanding between them.

water-base varnish

Because it is easier to use, faster to dry, and less toxic than alkyd varnish, water-base varnish has become a popular protective finish choice. Water-base varnishes are made with several kinds of binders; the strongest is urethane. For best results, apply two to three coats of varnish and sand between coats with very fine sandpaper, making sure to clean off the dust with a tack cloth.

A hardwood floor, pickled in pastel colors, is protected with a layer of polyurethane varnish. See pages 194–195 for instructions on pickling.

Color Matches (American Tradition colors) Floor: White, Blue Willow, and Del Coronado Dusty Rose

alkyd varnish

Alkyd varnish is more durable and higher gloss than the water-base version and is preferred for woodwork and furniture because it leaves no brush marks. It also provides the best results over faux finishes.

polyurethane

Polyurethane is the common term for an alkyd varnish that is formulated with a urethane-alkyd binder. It creates a shiny, thick coating that's very resistant to water, heat, alcohol, and scratching. Polyurethane is not appropriate over any work done with artist's oils. Allowing the proper drying time between coats is very important when you use polyurethane, so check the manufacturer's recommendations before working with it.

shellac

Shellac is a natural resin that is mixed with denatured alcohol and used as a finish and as a fast-drying primer. Shellac comes in several transparent colors: "clear" (also known as "white") and three shades of "orange"—"button" (the darkest), "garnet," and "amber" (the lightest). It also comes in various thicknesses, called cuts, with 1-pound-cut being the thinnest and 3-pound-cut the most common. Shellac can be used over bare or stained wood to provide a warm, flat finish that is especially attractive on antiques or faux-antiqued surfaces. It also can be used as a barrier between coats of incompatible finishes. Never use shellac on woodwork or furniture where alcoholic drinks may be spilled. Alcohol will leave a ring or eat through the finish.

natural oil finishes

Drying oils, such as linseed oil and tung oil, penetrate wood and add a natural sheen. They are best used on bare or stained wood. Apply them with a cloth and let them dry for several hours between applications.

wood **stains**

While paint is a popular choice for adding color to woodwork, stain or dye lets you add color without covering the natural grain of the wood. Stains and dyes come in colors—reds, yellows, blues, and greens— as well as wood tones.

Before selecting a color, be aware that each wood species has its own unique color and other characteristics that will affect how the trim takes a stain. Some woods, such as cherry, mahogany, and

A variety of bold wood color dyes applied to the fronts of cabinets and the floor creates a circus atmosphere in this lively kitchen.

Color Matches Ceiling: Valspar Mallow; wall: Earth Elements Open Plain

redwood, have a reddish hue; others—
poplar, pine, fir, and maple—have a more
yellow tone. (Most woods also change
color with prolonged exposure to light.)
These color characteristics also affect how
the wood appears with other colors, such
as wall paint. Some wood species pick
up stain much more readily than others,
affecting the final appearance as well.

Before covering large sections of wood,
test the stain or dye on a sample board.
Once you start the project, you can control the intensity of color with the amount
of pressure you apply to the wiping cloth,
as well as the number of coats you apply.
Seal with a protective finish (see page 67).

pigmented stain

A pigmented stain covers only the surface
of the wood, creating greater contrast
between its naturally light and dark areas.
Any time you want to accentuate both the
grain and the knots in the wood, a pigmented stain is a good choice. Apply stain
as evenly as possible to avoid patchy color
and brush marks.

wood dye

For a color that is very consistent, whether
applied to a softwood or a hardwood, use
a wood dye, available in water-base and
alcohol-base formulations. Wood dye is
absorbed into the fibrous structure of the
wood and changes its color. The color will
be darker on softwood
than on hardwood.
When using a dye,
make sure that the
wood is very clean,
with no grease or wax
on the surface to pre-
vent the dye from
being absorbed.

LOWE'S QUICK TIP

To see the final effect
of one versus two
coats, apply one coat
to your sample, let it
dry, and then apply a
second coat on just
half the board.

SAFETY PRECAUTIONS

While painting is one of the safest and easiest home improvement
projects for the average homeowner, you still need to exercise some
caution when working with paint. Here are some basic safety guidelines
to follow.

■ Wear a dust mask and safety goggles when you're sanding to keep
dust particles from getting in your lungs and eyes.

■ Be wary of plastic sheeting on the floor—it can be slippery. Canvas
or leak-resistant paper drop cloths may be a better choice. (See
page 74 for information on drop cloths.)

■ Carefully read the labels on paint cans for warnings about possible
hazards and follow all safety instructions provided.

■ Never smoke while painting or when using paint thinner (mineral
spirits) or any volatile solvent.

■ Keep all paint and paint products out of the reach of children
and pets.

■ Keep children and pets out of freshly painted rooms; paint fumes
can be especially harmful to pet birds.

■ Don't use or store paint products near a flame or heat source.

■ Always work with paint products in a well-ventilated area. Open
doors and windows and use exhaust fans. Excessive inhalation of
fumes from paints and solvents can result in dizziness, headaches,
fatigue, and nausea.

■ If you can't ventilate a room sufficiently, wear an approved respirator,
not just a dust mask.

■ Wear safety goggles when painting overhead or when using chemical
strippers or caustic cleaning compounds.

■ Wear latex gloves when staining or using alkyd paints or finishes to
protect your skin from strong solvents.

■ Inspect stepladders for sturdiness. Make sure that all four legs are
resting squarely on the floor and both cross braces are locked in
place. Never stand on the top step or the utility shelf. Never lean
away from a ladder; instead, get off and move it if you can't reach
a spot easily.

■ For scaffolding planks, use 2-by-10s no more than 12 feet long. If you
are placing the planks between two stepladders, position the ladders
so their steps are facing each other. Be sure that the planks are level.

■ Clean up promptly after painting and properly dispose of soiled rags
and paper towels. If you have used rags, sponges, or paper towels to
work with or to clean up oil-base or alkyd paint, paint thinner, or any
other flammable liquid, spread the materials to dry outdoors or in a
well-ventilated area away from children and pets; do not leave the
materials unattended overnight. Dispose of the materials according
to local ordinances.

Color Matches **Walls: base coat: American Tradition Husk Gold; top coat: Decorative Effects Lime Wash; ceiling and trim: American Tradition Parchment**

A pale lime glaze color-washed over the walls adds a patina of age to a contemporary living room—a perfect counterpoint to the sleek leather sofa and wood coffee table.

glazes

Most decorative painting techniques are done with glazes or washes (see the last two chapters). Some people use the term "glaze" when the paint base is alkyd, and the term "wash" when the paint base is latex. In this book, a "glaze" is any thinned paint—either alkyd or latex—that is translucent or transparent. The liquid used to thin the paint is called a medium. Latex glazes can be thinned with water or with a latex glazing liquid. Acrylic latex is thinned with acrylic glazing liquid and water, and acrylic artist's oils are thinned with water and a commercial transparent gel that is called acrylic medium. Alkyd paint is thinned with alkyd glazing liquid, paint thinner, and linseed oil for an added sheen.

Because of the popularity of decorative painting, you can now purchase commercially prepared translucent glazes with color already added (see page 64). As described on the opposite page, however, you can also make your own glaze to suit your specific needs. Your homemade glaze

can have whatever color or thickness you choose, although—unlike a commercial glaze—it may be too thin if you mix it incorrectly. The newer commercially prepared latex glazes are also formulated to stay workable longer and to retain color intensity, which are real advantages over ones that you mix yourself.

Alkyd glazes are the traditional medium of professional decorative painters because they stay wet and workable longer than latex or latex acrylic glazes and produce a durable and luminous finish. Mistakes are easy to correct—just dab on paint thinner and wipe off the glaze. Note, however, that handling alkyd paints and thinners requires care because of the chemicals and fumes involved. An alkyd glaze need not be used only over an alkyd base coat; it can also be applied over a latex base coat.

By contrast, a latex glaze is easy to prepare and clean up. Latex glazes' faster drying time can make them more challenging to use, however. Latex finishes also generally don't last as long as alkyd ones, although you can apply a clear coating to protect them.

LOWE'S QUICK TIP

To keep premixed oil colors from drying out, pour some linseed oil on top and seal the containers. When you're ready to paint, carefully pour the linseed oil into another container.

making your own glaze

It's not difficult to mix your own glaze. But since mixing glaze is not an exact science, you may need to experiment with the following formulas. Adding glazing liquid (available at Lowe's) increases the quantity of glaze without affecting the color or thinning the consistency. Adding paint thinner to alkyds or water to latex mixtures dilutes both color and consistency.

Alkyd Glaze

A good general recipe for beginners, this glaze stays wet even if you work slowly. For faster drying and a harder finish, use less glazing liquid and more paint thinner, and omit the linseed oil. The glaze tends to dry flat, so if you want more sheen, add linseed oil. It is a good glaze for color-washing, rubbing, dragging, stippling, rag rolling, ragging, flogging, and combing (see the last two chapters for projects using these techniques).

- 1 part alkyd paint
- 1 part alkyd glazing liquid
- 1 part paint thinner
- Small amount of linseed oil (approximately ½ cup per gallon of mixture)

Put the paint in a mixing container. Pour each of the other ingredients into the paint slowly as you stir.

Latex Glaze

You can vary this recipe so that water makes up anything from 10 to 90 percent of the mixture. The more paint you use, the more durable the finish. The more water, the more transparent the glaze and the lighter the color. Keep in mind, too, that latex paint is much darker when dry than when wet. This glaze is most suitable for color-washing, sponging, and limestone effects (see pages 140–144, 155–157, and 177–179 for projects using these techniques).

- 1 part latex paint
- 2 parts water

Put the paint in a mixing container. Pour the water into the paint slowly as you stir.

Acrylic Glaze

Mix this glaze in large or small quantities, as appropriate, for colorwashing, spattering, stamping, and stenciling (see the next two chapters for projects using these techniques).

- 2 parts latex acrylic paint
- 1 part acrylic glazing liquid
- 1 part water (approximately; see below)
- 2 to 4 ounces acrylic gel retarder per gallon (optional; available at art supply stores)

For a large quantity, first mix the acrylic paint and glazing liquid until the color is slightly darker than you want (it will lighten up with water). Gradually add the water until you get the consistency you want.

For a small quantity, first place the acrylic paint and the glazing liquid separately on an artist's palette. Using a palette knife, spread the paint toward the glazing liquid, mixing to get a color slightly darker than you want. Then transfer the mixture to a container and, while stirring, gradually add the water.

selecting tools for painting

JUST LIKE YOUR CHOICE OF PAINT, THE QUALITY OF THE TOOLS YOU SELECT will affect the ease and outcome of your painting project. Good-quality tools suited to the task and used the right way will make the job go faster and look more professional. Most painting projects require a few good basic brushes and at least one quality roller. Depending on your project, you may need other applicators or protective equipment.

brushes

A quality brush feels comfortable in your hand—not awkward or heavy. It should have flagged, or split, bristles set firmly in a metal ferrule with epoxy cement, not glue. The more flagged bristles there are, the more paint the brush can hold. Most bristles should be long—and thicker at the base than at the tip—but there should be a few short ones mixed in. Pull on the bristles to make sure none come out easily. Look for the new ergonomic brushes, designed to be held like a pencil for precision application and comfort.

For general purposes, you can get by nicely with three types of brushes: a 4-inch straight-edged brush for spreading paint on large surfaces, a 2- or 3-inch trim brush for painting woodwork, and a 1-inch angled sash brush for cutting in corners and detail work.

synthetic bristle brushes

Synthetic bristle brushes can be used with all paints, and should be used with latex paint. Polyester bristles keep their shape when immersed in water and perform well when painting warm surfaces, while nylon bristles are longer-lasting. A nylon-polyester blend combines both good shape retention and durability.

natural bristle brushes

Brushes with natural bristles should be used to apply alkyd paint and other finishes that clean up with paint thinner. Don't use them with latex paint or any water-base products, however, because natural bristles become limp when they soak up water.

foam brushes

Disposable foam brushes are handy for small jobs, quick touchups, and faux finishes. If you're bothered by the idea of adding them to the landfill, use a bristle brush instead and clean it thoroughly for reuse.

paint rollers and covers

Look for a roller with a heavy-gauge steel frame, an expandable wire roller cage, and a comfortable handle with a metal sleeve threaded to accommodate an extension pole. A 9-inch roller is a good choice for nearly all jobs. For some work you may prefer to use special rollers, such as a 3-inch one for small jobs, corners, and blending in touch-ups, or a hot-dog roller for decorative techniques. Don't bother with a roller shield, a device intended to minimize spattering. It's better to prevent spatter by avoiding excessive speed in rolling or improper roller nap thickness.

Choose a roller cover that is appropriate for the paint you're using and that has no obvious seams. Use a nylon cover for latex paint. For alkyd paint, use nylon and wool blend, lambskin, or mohair covers. The nap thickness on roller covers varies from $\frac{1}{16}$ inch to $1\frac{1}{4}$ inches. The smoother the surface you're painting, the shorter the nap you should use. Nap thicknesses of ¹⁄₁₆ to ¼ inch are appropriate for smooth plaster, wood, or metal surfaces. Use ⅜- to ¾-inch nap for semi-rough surfaces such as light-textured stucco, poured concrete, and rough wood. Use anything over ¾ inch for heavy stucco, brick, and concrete block.

Specialty covers with textured or raised surfaces can be used to create faux finishes such as rag-rolled patterns, fantasy wood grain, or various all-over patterns. But be aware that these can be frustrating to use. You can't reroll glaze with a textured tool, and it's nearly impossible to align adjacent passes or correct imperfections. You might want to reserve them for use on small items or defined areas, such as floorboards or door components.

pad **applicators**

A pad applicator with a replaceable pad can be useful for painting corners and edges. As with roller covers, use nylon pads with latex paints; nylon and wool blend, lambskin, or mohair pads are best for alkyd paints. With pads, apply paint in one direction only.

Brushes, rollers, and pad applicators come in an assortment of sizes, shapes, and materials.

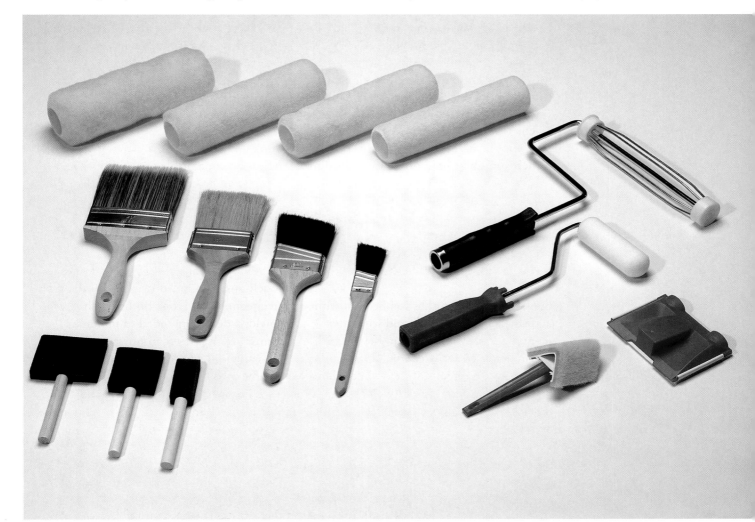

other paint equipment

paint bucket and grid A 5-gallon bucket fitted with a metal grid is the best container for primer or base-coat paint for a large area.

paint tray Paint trays come in plastic and in metal. Disposable liners make cleanup easier. They are good for jobs where you won't use a lot of paint or only want to paint a small section at a time. A plastic tray with a lid lets you put projects on hold for hours at a time without the paint drying out.

caulking gun When you need to fill a gap between wood trim and a wall, a caulking gun does the job quickly and uniformly. An inexpensive latex or vinyl caulk will generally work fine, but use all-acrylic or siliconized acrylic caulk where water or movement is an issue.

drop cloths These are available in canvas, paper, and plastic. Canvas is the best, but it's expensive and cumbersome. Plain paper will protect against splatters, but not a large amount of spilled paint. Less expensive than canvas is paper fiber cloth with a synthetic moisture-barrier backing. Plastic works well over furniture, but can be slippery on floors. Look for pre-taped drop cloths for additional convenience.

edge guide When you're painting baseboards, this handy device offers quick, portable protection for floors and carpets.

extension pole An extension pole is helpful for rolling paint on ceilings. One that telescopes allows you to change the length of the pole with a quick twist.

latex gloves Latex gloves are thin enough to allow flexibility yet sturdy enough to protect your skin from chemicals. Always wear them for projects with oil-base finishes.

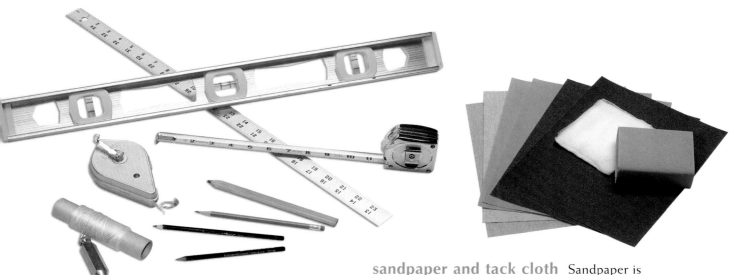

measuring devices
For measuring and marking, a variety of rulers, tape measures, chalk lines, blackboard chalk, and pencils should be on hand. Use a level to ensure level horizontal lines and a plumb bob for vertical lines that are perfectly perpendicular to a level surface. For marking walls, use a water-soluble lead pencil.

sandpaper and tack cloth
Sandpaper is needed to smooth surfaces after patching or between coats. For large flat surfaces, a sanding block—to which you attach sandpaper—eases the job. A lint-free tack cloth treated with a sticky resin coating captures and removes dust from the surface.

scrapers
A putty knife, taping knife, broad knife, and hook-blade scraper are all useful tools for scraping and doing repair jobs on damaged walls or ceilings.

painter's masking tape
Painter's masking tape is invaluable for a good paint job. Brown paper painter's masking tape is 3 inches wide and has one sticky edge; it provides inexpensive all-purpose protection for adjacent surfaces. Blue masking tape, which is "low-tack," is better for masking delicate surfaces and hardware and is less likely to lift up paint.

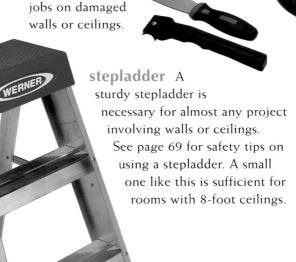

stepladder
A sturdy stepladder is necessary for almost any project involving walls or ceilings. See page 69 for safety tips on using a stepladder. A small one like this is sufficient for rooms with 8-foot ceilings.

decorative painting tools

ALTHOUGH THERE ARE NUMEROUS SPECIALTY BRUSHES AND ROLLERS AVAILABLE for decorative painting, you really don't need many of them for the techniques featured in this book. Use each project's "Tools and Materials" list as a guide when you assemble your gear, and don't hesitate to work with the inexpensive chip brushes and foam brushes that are frequently specified. When house painter's, specialty, or artist's brushes are called for, however, use the best quality you can afford.

artist's brushes These flat, round, and angled specialty brushes are essential for many faux finishes, as well as for adding details to stenciling and for general touchup. Script liners and fan brushes are used for graining. Instead of throwing out worn or inexpensive artist's brushes, save them to mix glazes.

fabrics Burlap is used to make veins for faux mahogany. Cotton-knit rags, also called jersey rags, are used to rub glazes. They may be sold in plastic bags or 5-pound boxes. Buy the jersey (smooth-knit) type, not the ribbed variety. Cheesecloth can be substituted for cotton rags to rub glazes. It is packaged both precut and in continuous lengths.

chip brush Inexpensive and versatile, chip brushes are used to apply glaze as well as to soften—and they're much cheaper than the badger-hair softening brushes traditionally used in faux finishing. You can also use them to apply glaze to mouldings.

flogger A long-bristled horsehair brush used to create "pores" in wood graining, this brush can be expensive. You can also flog with a standard house painter's brush, although the effect may not be as accurate.

curved painter's tool This handy tool has a crescent blade for scraping excess glaze or paint off a roller. It can also be used to open paint cans and to scrape inside corners.

graining combs Used for combing and for fantasy wood graining, graining combs have either rubber or metal teeth, which may be even or graduated in length. Each creates a different pattern in a different scale.

eraser tool Also called color shapers, these angled erasers with paintbrush-like handles are available in several sizes. They are good for removing fine lines of glaze in wood graining and faux malachite.

mottler This small, square brush is used for applying metal leaf.

plumb bob Useful for many home-repair projects besides painting, this weighted guide is used to establish straight vertical lines for such techniques as vertical striping and combing.

rubber stamps
Available at Lowe's as well as craft and stationery stores, stamps can be used with glazes, alone, or with other paint techniques.

sea sponges Natural sea sponges are used for sponging and to create a limestone effect. The larger the pores and more jagged the edges, the more open the decorative effect will be.

softening brush A softening brush is used to mute or soften details such as veins in graining or overall effects such as colorwashing.

stippling brush This large, short brush, made with hog-hair or horsehair bristles, is designed to be pounced rather than brushed over a surface. Several sizes are available.

stencil brushes These blunt-cut, cylindrical brushes made with hog-hair bristles are used to pounce or swirl paint onto a surface through a stencil. Their handles are usually short, though European stencil brushes are sometimes long-handled.

veiner A veiner is a long-haired natural bristle brush used to create veins for wood graining and marble.

buying your paint

IN ADDITION TO SELECTING THE TYPE OF PAINT YOU'LL USE, YOU NEED TO decide on the exact color and quantity to buy. You don't want to end up with the wrong color, have too little paint to complete your job, or be left with gallons of extra paint.

Paint chips help you select color, but be aware that the color on a paint chip will appear more intense when it's applied to the walls.

selecting color

If you haven't done so already, consult the first two chapters for ideas on picking your basic color scheme. Many paint companies also offer "mistake-proof" palettes that allow you to mix colors in a room with confidence. And Lowe's provides a number of ways to help you pick a color scheme (see opposite page).

But even with all this assistance, you should still test color samples on your walls. How do they absorb and reflect the light in the room? How do they blend with your existing furnishings? When the chip you love becomes four walls of color, will you hate it?

Start by bringing home a range of paint chips in different values of your chosen colors. (Don't worry if your samples come from different manufacturers. Lowe's Paint Sales Specialists can computer-match color from any paint chip or even a piece of fab-

Brush-outs show how paint colors might appear in different room situations, as well as how colors will look from one room to another.

Color Match American Tradition Citrus Orange

ric and duplicate it in a Lowe's brand of paint.) Hold the chips up in several places in the room—in the middle of a wall that faces a window, on a wall with no direct light, and in corners. Look carefully for the undertones, which will appear much stronger once the paint covers the entire wall. (Is it a pink beige or a gray beige? An orange-based yellow or a green-based yellow?) Because paint tends to look one or two values darker once it's actually on the walls, experts recommend sticking with the middle tones of a paint strip. If you choose too light a color, though, the result will lack character.

the brush-out

The next step is to do the equivalent of test-driving the paint. A "brush-out" involves covering a 3-foot-square area of a room with color, by applying paint either to a wall or to a large portable surface such as poster board. Buy the smallest quantity of each color you can; usually this will be a quart, but some paint formulas can only be made in gallon size.

The best way to do a brush-out is to paint the walls themselves—preferably both walls at a corner, so you can see how the color changes on different planes. It may look as though you used two different paints, since each surface receives a different amount of light. Alternatively, you can paint a 3-foot-square piece of foam core or poster board and move it around the room. If you plan to use a multicolor paint scheme—perhaps adjoining walls in different colors—brush the colors next to each other in the area where you will paint them.

Examine the brush-out carefully day and night, in both natural and artificial light. Stand back and block out the surrounding area with your hands, as if framing a picture, and squint. Don't forget to test wall colors against any new ceiling and trim hues as well; the ceiling will appear darker because it gets less light. You may have to do brush-outs with three or more colors to find the right one.

estimating paint needs

To figure out how much paint to buy, you must know the square footage of the area you intend to paint. Here's how. (You can also use the Paint Calculator at www.lowes. com to estimate paint quantity.)

First measure the width of each wall, add the widths together, and then multiply by the height of the walls. For a rectangular ceiling, multiply the two sides.

Next, estimate how much of the room contains surfaces that won't be painted, such as a fireplace, windows, doors, and wallpaper, or areas you'll paint separately, such as woodwork. If those surfaces add up to more than 10 percent of the room, subtract that amount from your total. Double your requirement if you're going to apply two coats.

As a rule, the amount of trim in a room —including window trim, door trim, baseboards, and ceiling moulding—is roughly proportionate to the amount of wall space by a 1-to-4 ratio. For every gallon of paint for the walls, then, you'll need about a quart for the trim.

Once you know the square footage of the area you'll be painting, refer to the spreading rate printed on the paint can to see approximately how many square feet it will cover. Buy enough paint for the job plus a little left over for future touchups.

preparing surfaces for painting

THE KEY TO A SUCCESSFUL PAINT JOB IS PLANNING AND PREPARATION. BEFORE you get out your brushes and open the paint cans, make sure you have easy access to all your walls and ceilings, and cover all surfaces you want to protect from spatters. Your walls and ceilings will need to be clean and smooth, free of any obvious blemishes, which will become more obvious under new paint.

arranging the room

Move as much furniture and accessories as possible out of the room. Push heavy furniture into the middle of the room and cover it with drop cloths. Protect the flooring with drop cloths.

Remove everything you can from the walls and ceilings. Unscrew and remove any duct covers. Turn off the power to the room and remove electrical faceplates and any fixtures. If you can't take down a light fixture, loosen the ceiling or wall plate and tie a plastic garbage bag around both the plate and the fixture to protect them from paint spatters. If you're painting doors or window frames, remove any hardware, marking the pieces so you can replace them correctly later.

smoothing the walls and ceiling

If your surfaces are not entirely smooth, new paint won't adhere well to them, so you'll need to scrape and sand chipped and peeling paint. Dents, cracks, and holes should be repaired.

You'll be happier with your paint project if you take the time to cover floors, furniture, and other surfaces completely.

scraping and stripping

The trick with scraping is to scrape hard enough to remove the paint, but not so hard that you dig into the surface. The best scrapers have edges that can be sharpened with a metal file. A broad knife does a fast job on large areas; a hook-blade scraper is more convenient for small areas. A wire brush is effective for removing light flaking.

In some cases, you may need to remove the old paint entirely. The easiest way to strip old paint is with a commercial liquid paint stripper. Look for one of the newer environmentally friendly products that do not contain methylene chloride or other harsh solvents, and are biodegradable, non-flammable, and noncombustible. Follow the application directions on the container carefully.

If your house was built before 1978, there may be lead in the older coats of paint. Refer to page 82 for information on how to handle lead-base paint.

In most cases, it is best to remove wall-paper before you paint. However, you can paint over a single layer of wallpaper in good condition. (Note that once you paint over wallpaper, it will be almost impossible to remove.) If you want to paint over it, test the paint in an inconspicuous area and wait a few days to see if the pattern bleeds through or the paper begins to peel. Always prime before painting.

Never try painting over two or more wallpaper layers. To remove wallpaper, saturate and soften it using a sponge soaked in warm water, and then scrape it off; if the paper is thick, score it with rough sandpaper before soaking it. If the paper won't come off, try renting a steam stripper. Remove any bits of glue with an abrasive cleaner. The wall should be completely dry before painting.

Above: **A wire brush is effective at scratching away small areas of flaking paint.**

Left: **Use a broad knife or putty knife to scrape away layers of old paint.**

A sanding block helps you avoid creating dips or low spots in the wood.

DEALING WITH LEAD-BASE PAINT

If you are repainting in a house built before 1978, layers of lead-base paint may be hiding under your current finish. Lead-base paint can be on any surface, including the walls, ceilings, doors, windows, trim, floors, radiators, stairways, railings, furniture,and even electrical plate covers. The paint poses no threat if it is covered and left undisturbed. But removing it, sanding it, scraping it, or patching or demolishing a surface that has a lead-base coat could expose you, your family, and your pets to poisoning from lead dust and paint chips. Lead poisoning can cause serious, long-term harm.

If you suspect the presence of lead-base paint in your home, have the paint tested by a qualified professional before you start your project. (The results of do-it-yourself testing kits are not as reliable.) To find an inspector, contact your local health department or the National Lead Information Center at 800/424-LEAD.

If an inspector discovers lead-base paint in your home, request a copy of the EPA booklet, "Reducing Lead Hazards When Remodeling Your Home." If you follow all of the work practices and safety precautions provided in the booklet, you can remove old paint yourself. An environmentally safe paint removal paste called Peel Away 1 is especially formulated for removing oil-base lead paint (contact Dumond Chemicals, 212/869-6350; www.dumondchemicals.com). An infrared heat tool called the Silent Paint Remover is also a safe removal option (contact Viking Sales, 585/271-7169; www.silentpaintremover.netfirms.com). Otherwise, you should hire a qualified professional to handle this part of the job, making sure your walls are completely stripped and clean before you continue with the painting process. Consider having the inspector return after the work is done to ensure that the house is clear of any lead dust contamination.

sanding and deglossing

Interestingly, sandpaper can be used both to smooth and to roughen. Once you have scraped a surface, you need to sand it lightly; this will remove irregularities in the surface—make it smooth. You should also sand newly patched areas for the same reason. Any glossy surface or bare wood should be sanded with fine-grit sandpaper to roughen it, to give the surface "tooth" that the new paint can adhere to.

You can use sandpaper on both latex and alkyd paints. After sanding, use a tack cloth to remove any dust from all surfaces and then vacuum the room. Liquid deglosser or trisodium phosphate (TSP) can also be used on alkyds; these are convenient for hard-to-sand areas. If you use a liquid deglosser, which is a strong solvent, or TSP, always ventilate the room well and wear a respirator, rubber gloves, and safety goggles. Rinse the wall thoroughly after deglossing.

cleaning

Even if it's not necessary to strip, sand, or degloss the surfaces you plan to paint, accumulated dust, dirt, or grease should be removed. Use a sponge and mild household detergent for dirt and dust. Grease, oil, and mildew require a stronger cleanser and a scrub brush. You can use TSP to get out stubborn stains, or create a simple cleaning solution with ammonia mixed with an equal amount of water or one part bleach to three parts water. Bleach is especially effective on mildew. Allow all surfaces to dry for at least 24 hours before painting.

masking

Unless you have an extremely steady hand, it's a good idea to protect surfaces immediately adjacent to where you'll be painting by covering them with masking tape. Masking tape is also useful for keeping a crisp edge between two types or colors of paint.

Be sure to use the right masking tape for the job and to choose an adhesion level—there are at least six—appropriate for the surface it is covering. Generally, 3-inch brown paper painter's tape is suitable; it has one sticky edge you apply adjacent to the area you'll be painting. Blue low-tack tape is good for delicate surfaces, since it won't cause damage when it is pulled away. To ensure a tight seal, run a putty knife along the tape.

You can also protect surfaces with pre-taped plastic drop cloths, which can be used to cover larger wall areas, and painter's plastic, which adheres with static electricity and is good for protecting woodwork or wallpaper. For window corners, look for a roll of 2-inch masking corners that you can press onto the glass.

Some masking tape can be left on surfaces for a while without causing problems upon removal. However, it's generally a good idea to remove masking tape promptly so that the adhesive doesn't damage the walls, lift the new paint, or leave a residue. To remove it, unpeel one end, fold it back approximately parallel to the painted surface, and pull gently—if you hold the tape perpendicular to the painted surface, you're more likely to pull off paint along with the tape. If it is difficult to remove the tape, you may be able to loosen it by warming it with a hair dryer.

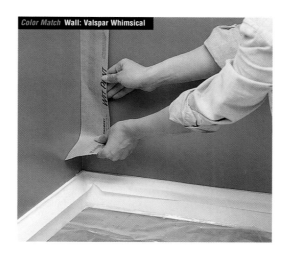

Color Match Wall: Valspar Whimsical

Left: **Apply the sticky edge of the tape adjacent to the area you'll be painting.**

Below: **To remove tape without pulling off paint, fold it back so it's almost parallel to the wall.**

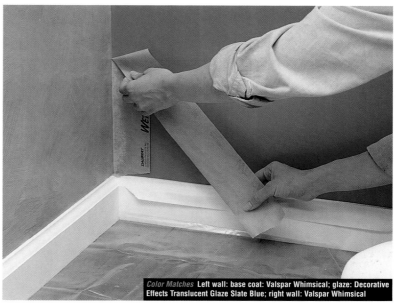

Color Matches **Left wall: base coat: Valspar Whimsical; glaze: Decorative Effects Translucent Glaze Slate Blue; right wall: Valspar Whimsical**

making repairs

SMALL HOLES, CRACKS, AND OTHER MINOR SURFACE DAMAGE ARE RELATIVELY
easy problems to fix yourself. For extensive damage, you may need to call in a professional.
Large cracks in a wall or ceiling may indicate uneven settling of your foundation. If you
can fit the tip of your little finger into a crack, consider having the foundation inspected.

After you have made any repairs, sand and clean the surface. In most cases, you will
also need to seal the area with a primer before painting.

patching nail holes and cracks

Use your finger or a putty knife to fill nail
holes or very small cracks with joint compound—or wood filler, if you're patching
wood. Before patching other small holes
and cracks, brush them clean and dampen
the surface. Using a putty knife, apply a
layer of joint compound or wood filler.
After patching any area, smooth it and
spot-prime.

patching small open holes

For a small hole larger than a nail hole,
cut two lengths of self-adhesive mesh joint
tape that's wider than the hole. Center one
piece over the hole and press it into the
wall. Center the other piece over the hole
to form an X with the first one and press it
in place. Then, using a putty knife, cover
the mesh with one or more layers of joint
compound. When the material is dry, sand
and spot-prime.

Color Match **Wall: American Tradition Imperial Blue**

Color Match **Wall: American Tradition Pink Mirage**

Above: Patch nail holes
with joint compound.

Right: Mesh tape makes
patching small holes fast
and easy.

patching **larger holes** in plaster

Unless you have a very textured plaster surface, making seamless repairs in walls constructed of plaster over wood lath requires a certain amount of time and patience. If the damage is extensive, you may want to hire a professional rather than do the repair yourself.

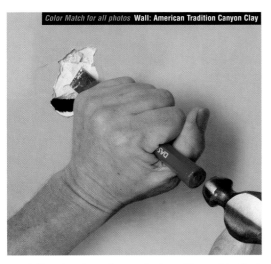

Color Match for all photos **Wall: American Tradition Canyon Clay**

1 Knock out any loose plaster with a cold chisel and ball-peen hammer. Clean out the plaster in and behind the lath to provide a surface to which the new plaster can adhere. Brush the area clean and dampen it with a sponge for better adhesion.

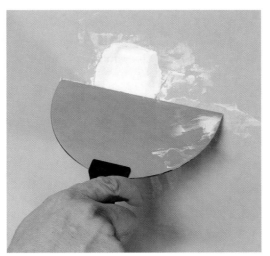

2 If the hole is smaller than 2 inches across, fill it with a single layer of patching compound and finish as described in Step 4. For larger holes, use three layers. For the first layer, work in from the outer edges with a 6-inch broad knife, filling about half the hole depth. Make sure to work the material through the gaps in the lath.

3 Score the patch with a nail to provide a rough surface for the next coat, then allow it to dry. Moisten the patch, then apply a second layer of patching compound, not quite filling the complete depth of the hole. Score the patch; let it dry.

4 Apply the final coat, feathering the edges an inch or so beyond the edges of the hole. Scrape a straightedge across the wet finish coat to remove any excess material. When the patch is dry, sand and spot-prime.

patching **larger holes** in drywall

One of the simplest ways to patch holes in drywall that are too large to be mended with mesh joint tape (see page 84) is with a drywall repair kit that uses special clips to secure the patch to the wall. These kits are available at Lowe's.

After you have screwed the patch to the clips, finish the seams and cover the clips as for finishing drywall (see opposite page).

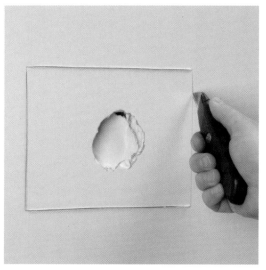

1 Start by cutting out the damaged area to form a rectangular hole with clean edges. Use a drywall saw or make a series of progressively deeper cuts with a utility knife.

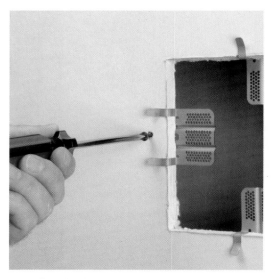

2 Slip the drywall repair clips onto the edges of the hole and screw them into place. Be sure to drive the screw heads slightly below the surface of the drywall.

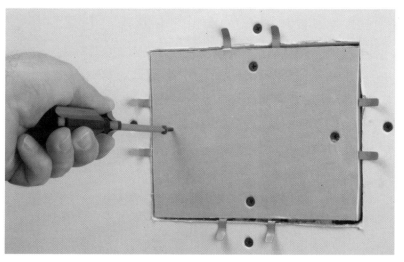

3 Cut a drywall patch to fit the hole. Drive screws through the patch and into the clips, driving the screw heads slightly below the surface of the drywall. Press the "ears" of the clips into the drywall.

finishing drywall

Whenever the surface of drywall has been marred—whether by a repair or by other damage—you need to close up the rent in the paper and restore a smooth surface.

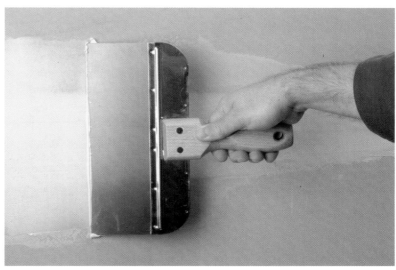

2 Let this coat dry completely (typically, overnight). Then sand it lightly and apply two more coats in the same way, using a wider knife with each coat. Work the compound gently away from the paper tape to feather it for a smooth transition.

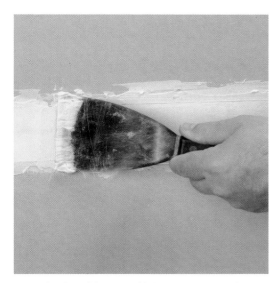

1 Apply a thin coat of joint compound using a putty knife, then press in a length of paper tape. Immediately apply a skim coat of joint compound and draw the knife over the surface, making sure it is flat and that there are no bubbles. Cover any nail or screw heads with joint compound.

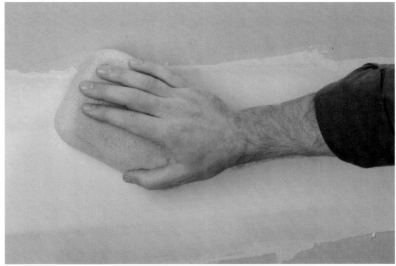

3 Allow the final coat to dry completely, then smooth with medium-grit sandpaper, followed by fine-grit sandpaper or a sanding screen. For a final smoothing, use a damp sponge, rather than sandpaper. Seal the drywall with a latex primer.

basic painting techniques

ONCE YOUR WALLS, CEILING, AND trim are smooth, clean, and free of blemishes, it's time to plan the painting job itself. By following a well-planned painting sequence, you can avoid splattering paint onto newly painted surfaces or inadvertently touching a just-painted edge. Here are some general rules of thumb.

If you are using stains or clear finishes on woodwork, apply them first. When the finish is completely dry, mask all trim adjacent to the walls and ceilings you will be painting.

Prime any surfaces that need a first coat (see page 60). Your primer should cover the area completely, but it doesn't have to be as neat as the finish coat. Do the ceiling first, then the walls.

When the primer is dry, paint the ceiling. Then paint the walls, starting from the top and working your way down. If you used a good-quality primer, you can probably cover surfaces in a single coat of premium paint. However, if you're painting over a darker color, you may need to apply two coats.

Finally, brush paint on any trim as needed. Start with the ceiling moulding, followed by any other horizontal trim, then the baseboards. You can either leave the window trim, door trim, and cabinets for last, or paint them just before the baseboards.

LOWE'S QUICK TIP

If you are doing a job that requires more than one can of paint, it is a good idea to "box"—or mix—your paint to avoid any color discrepancy from one can to the next. To box paint, simply pour two or more cans of the same color into a 5-gallon bucket and stir.

painting with a **brush**

Some professionals prefer painting entire walls and ceilings with brushes because they produce a smoother, less porous finish. But brushing is very time-consuming. A faster, more commonly used technique is to use a brush to "cut in" the borders of large areas and to paint trim. Most of each surface can then be painted with a roller. When you paint with a brush, never work directly from a paint can, if you can help it. Instead, pour the paint into a large bucket and stir it.

loading the brush

Prepare your brush by rolling the bristles between your palms to remove any loose bristles; then shake the brush vigorously. Dip one-third of the length of the bristles into the stirred paint, then lift and dip again two or three times to saturate the bristles. If this is the first time you're loading the brush, gently stir the paint with it so that the bristles spread slightly; don't do this when reloading. Lift the brush straight up, letting excess paint drip into the bucket. Gently slap both sides of the brush against the inside of the bucket two or

Color Matches (American Tradition colors) Wall: Orchid Pearl; trim: White; on brush: Berkshire Blue

To remove excess paint from a brush, slap it against the inside of the container, rather than scraping it against the lip.

three times. Don't wipe the brush against the lip of the bucket; this can cause the bristles to separate into clumps, leaving too little paint on the brush.

cutting in with a brush

Before you paint a whole wall or ceiling, whether you will be rolling or brushing it, cut in the edges with a 2- to 3-inch trim brush. (Use a foam brush for glaze.) If the wall and ceiling will be different colors, you can mask the edge of whichever surface you are not painting, or use an edge guide to keep paint from straying.

If you're using flat or eggshell latex paint, you can cut in the entire room before painting the open spaces. For semigloss or gloss latex or for any alkyd paint, you'll get better results if you cut in

a small section and then fill it in before moving to the next section. Do not let the edge of one section dry before starting another, or you'll get a demarcation line.

If you're using the same paint for the ceiling and wall, you can paint several inches out from the ceiling-to-wall connection on both sides. If you're using different colors or types of paint, cut in and paint the ceiling before you paint the walls.

For a ceiling, cut in first where the ceiling meets the wall, working all the way around the ceiling. Then cut in around any hanging fixtures.

For a wall, cut in first along the ceiling, then the vertical edges and above the baseboard, next around door and window frames, then around any light fixtures, outlets, or other fixed items on the wall.

Color Matches on both photos (American Tradition colors) Wall: White; on brush: Berkshire Blue

1 When you cut in, position the brush about two brush lengths from a corner and paint toward the corner using long, overlapping strokes.

2 When that section is done, start about two brush lengths from where you began before and blend the paint into the wet edge. Continue in this manner until you reach the next corner and then repeat this process along each edge until you have worked around the entire wall.

LOWE'S QUICK TIP

Dampening the bristles before you paint will help latex go on more evenly. Wipe off any excess moisture before loading the brush to prevent drips.

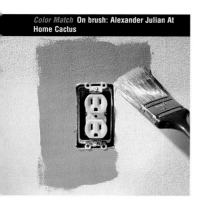

Always remove receptacle covers before cutting in around outlets or light switches. Be careful not to paint the switch or outlet itself.

painting whole surfaces with a brush

To paint an entire surface with a brush, first cut in the edges. Then spread paint smoothly and evenly over a 3-foot-square area, holding the brush at about a 45-degree angle to the surface, gradually reducing pressure at the end of the stroke. Instead of wrapping your hand around the paintbrush handle, hold the brush with your thumb on one side and your four fingers spread on the ferrule. This grip gives you good control of the brush and allows you to swivel and angle the brush throughout the brushstroke, without moving the rest of your body.

Paint toward a dry area and then back into a wet edge. This helps avoid lap marks. On smooth surfaces, direct the final strokes all one way, but on rough surfaces, vary the direction. When painting with a semigloss or high-gloss finish, make the final brushstrokes away from the light source in the room. The tiny ridges that a brush leaves won't be as pronounced. For wood, paint parallel to the grain. When the first 3-foot-square area is filled, soften the brush marks by running the brush, unloaded, very lightly over the wet paint. Begin the next area a few inches from the last finished area. When the new section is completed, brush into the previously finished one, blending the overlap.

When you need to paint railings or narrow chair spindles, a painter's mitt can do the job more quickly than a paintbrush. With the thick soft mitt on your hand, dip it into a paint tray. Then grasp the railing; slide the mitt over the surface.

The grip shown here is the most comfortable way to hold a brush, and it allows you to move the brush efficiently.

painting with a **roller**

Use a brush to cut in the edges of any surface before you use a roller. The process of rolling on paint is essentially the same whether you're painting a ceiling or a wall. The object is to create a coat that appears seamless.

loading the roller

Before you use a new napped roller, you should remove the excess lint. Unroll a length of 3-inch masking tape (regular tape, not painter's). Place the roller cover on a roller frame and roll it back and forth over the tape. This step is not necessary with a foam roller.

Depending on the size of your job, you can paint from either a paint tray or a 5-gallon bucket fitted with a wire mesh grid. If you're using a tray, pour in just enough paint to fill the reservoir. Dip the roller into the reservoir, then roll up and down the textured part of the tray to distribute paint and saturate the nap. For larger jobs, a bucket is more efficient. Pour 1 or 2 gallons of paint into the bucket. Dip the roller in. Run the roller back and forth on the mesh grid to spread the paint evenly and squeeze out the excess. Whether you use a bucket or a tray, the roller should be full, but not dripping, when you go to work.

rolling the ceiling

When painting a ceiling, use an extension pole so you won't have to stand directly under the section you are painting. This minimizes your chances of getting spattered or dripped on. (The alternative, working on a ladder, forces you to move up and down constantly to change its position.)

Color Matches (American Tradition colors) Wall: White; on roller: Orchid Pearl

Color Matches (American Tradition colors) Wall: Orchid Pearl; trim: White; on roller: Berkshire Blue

Top: Remove excess paint from a roller by rolling it up and down a metal grid.

Above: When excess paint collects on the end of a roller, blot it off on a paper towel or rag.

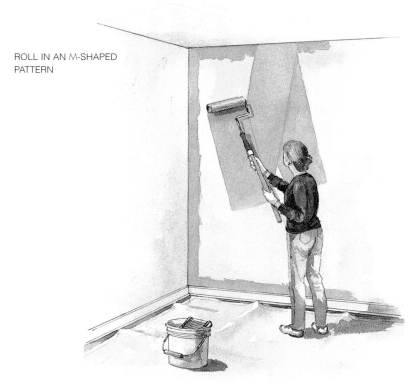

ROLL IN AN M-SHAPED PATTERN

Always work across the ceiling's shorter dimension, doing a small 3-foot-square section at a time. Start in a corner and paint diagonally in a large M shape across the section, then roll back and forth to distribute the paint evenly over the area. Reload the roller as needed; roll slowly. When you have completed the whole width, from one wall to the opposite one, roll the unloaded roller in one long straight stroke along the edge adjacent to the unpainted area. Along the walls, roll as close to the edge of the ceiling as possible to cover any differences in texture between the cutting-in brush marks and the roller marks.

rolling the walls

The most efficient way to cover a wall is to start in one corner (left if you're right-handed, right if you're left-handed) and roll on the paint in a large M-shaped pattern, working in 3- by 4-foot sections.

Load your roller with paint and off-load the excess. Roll diagonally upward first, keeping a light, even pressure on the roller. Without reloading or lifting it, roll down diagonally to form the first point of the M. Still without reloading or lifting the roller, roll up and down to form the second point of the M. Avoid spinning the roller as you lift it off the painted surface. Next, roll back and forth to distribute the paint evenly over the area and fill in the M. You may need to reload the roller.

FILL IN THE M-SHAPED PATTERN

Once you've finished the first section, make the next M shape below it. When you've completed one full length of wall, top to bottom, roll the unloaded roller in one long straight stroke along the edge adjacent to the unpainted area. Do the same close to the corner of the wall to conceal the differences in texture between the cutting-in brush marks and the roller marks. Then repeat the process for the next length of wall.

rolling on glaze

When you roll on glaze, it should cover the surface evenly and without drips, but still be wet enough for use in faux finishing. Because glaze is thinner than paint, it tends to run when you apply it. Minimize dripping by scraping off the excess glaze with a curved painter's tool after loading your roller.

To roll glaze on a wall, first cut in the corners with a foam brush (see page 89). With the roller, start at the ceiling and work down to the baseboard, rolling on one roller width at a time. Without reloading the roller, reroll the applied glaze until the coverage is uniform. If you are painting a small area, you may have to wait a few minutes for the glaze to set before you start decorative techniques such as ragging off, dragging, or combing (see "Decorative Effects for Walls," pages 138–181).

working with a partner

For any decorative technique that involves covering a relatively large portion of the surface with glaze and then removing some of it, consider working with a partner. Many of these techniques require you to work quickly so that you can seamlessly blend one section with the previous one before the glaze dries. When you work with a partner, one of you can roll on the glaze and the other can begin the decorative technique. For working together to be successful, you need to coordinate your pace of work with each other carefully. Depending upon the technique and the height of the wall, the person rolling on the glaze may need to take breaks so the other one can catch up.

ONE ROLLS, ONE APPLIES
DECORATIVE TECHNIQUE

LOWE'S QUICK TIP

To minimize spattering, use a roller cover that has the right nap for the texture of your surface (see page 73), roll off the excess paint every time you load your roller, and don't work too quickly.

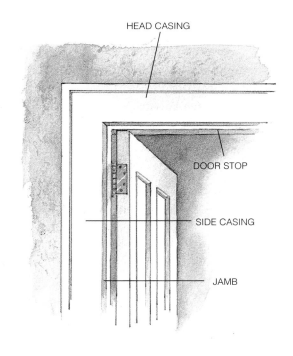

HEAD CASING

DOOR STOP

SIDE CASING

JAMB

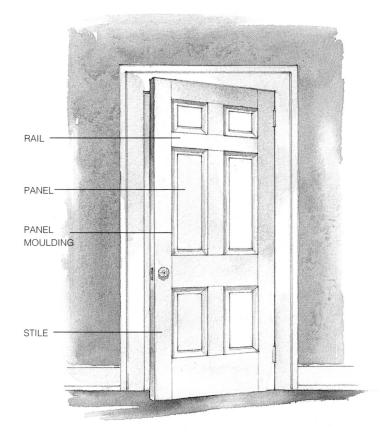

RAIL

PANEL

PANEL
MOULDING

STILE

painting **doors**

You may find it easier to paint a door by removing it from its opening and laying it at an angle against a wall or horizontally across a pair of sawhorses. To remove a door from its opening, slip the hinge pins out—the bottom one first—but don't unscrew the hinges. Whether you paint a door on or off its hinges, the painting sequence is exactly the same.

First mask the hinges to protect them from paint spatters. If your door has an inset panel, you should paint it with a brush. For flat doors, you can roll on the paint and then brush it out in the direction of the grain.

Always work from the top down. On a door with one or more inset panels, start by painting the mouldings around the panels, working from the outside in. Paint the horizontal rails first, then the vertical stiles. Use the tips of the bristles, unloaded, to pull the paint away from edges and corners, where it has a tendency to collect.

If a door separates two rooms painted in different colors, match the color of its latch edge to the room the door opens into and the color of its hinge edge to the room the door opens away from.

When painting the trim and door frame, begin with the head casing and work down the side casings. If the door opens away from the room, paint the jamb and the two surfaces of the door stop visible from the room. If the door opens into the room, paint the jamb and the door side of the door stop. Don't rehang or close the door until all the paint is completely dry.

painting **windows**

Painting the narrow components of a wood window takes a steady hand and the right brush—an angled sash brush that can reach neatly into corners. If you don't happen to have a steady hand, cover all the edges of the glass with masking tape to shield them. Resist the temptation to work quickly without masking, thinking you'll scrape off excess paint later, since scraping can permanently scratch the glass. However, do let a tiny edge of the paint overlap onto the glass. This will seal the finish to it so that condensation forming on the glass won't get under the paint and cause it to peel. Don't leave tape too long on windows that are in the sun, as the tape may bond to the glass.

Begin painting with the head casing, then paint down the sides. Next paint the stool, and finish with the apron.

double-hung windows

If the sashes of a double-hung window are removable, lift them out, lay them on a table, and paint them. Be prepared to leave the sashes out long enough to dry thoroughly. If they aren't removable, you'll need to raise and lower them as needed to reach all window parts. Leave them slightly open until they're dry.

Paint the top sash first. If the window has small glass panes, begin with the hori-zontal muntins, then work on the vertical ones. Next, paint the exposed parts of the stiles, the top rail, and the bottom rail, in that order. Then paint the bottom sash as you did the top one.

casement windows

First paint any vertical muntins and then any horizontal ones. Next, paint the top rails, the bottom rails, and the stiles, in that order.

LOWE'S QUICK TIP

No matter what kind of window you have, do not paint the jamb. Paint could cause the window to stick later. Once the window is painted, wax a wood jamb with floor wax; leave other materials bare.

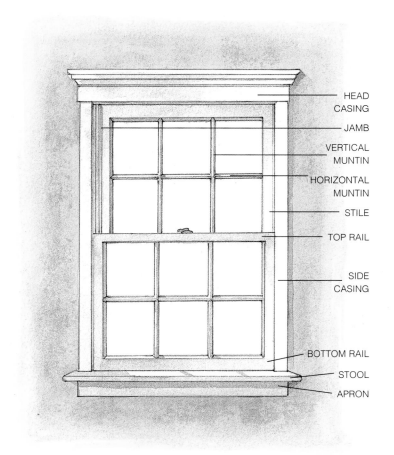

HEAD CASING

JAMB

VERTICAL MUNTIN

HORIZONTAL MUNTIN

STILE

TOP RAIL

SIDE CASING

BOTTOM RAIL

STOOL

APRON

CLEAN AND SAND CABINETS

PAINT FRAMES FIRST

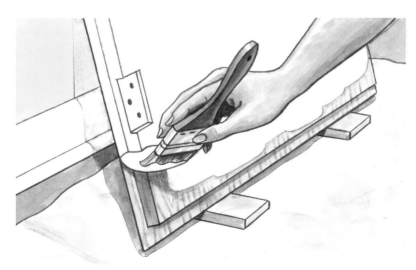

PAINT DOOR BACKS

painting cabinets

A fresh coat of paint on a set of cabinets can add years to its life. However, not all cabinets can be painted. Wood-veneer, solid wood, and metal cabinets take paint well, but cabinets with face frames covered in plastic laminate or melamine cannot be painted because paint will not bond properly to those surfaces. While you can brush or spray-paint cabinets, rolling is fast and works well on large surfaces. A short 4- to 6-inch foam roller will let you cover the face frames with a single stroke and quickly handle wider doors.

Remove all hardware, doors, and drawers from the cabinets; mark them with masking tape labels to make it easy to replace them properly when you're done painting. If you want to use new handles after you paint, fill and sand the holes left by the old ones.

Thoroughly clean and prepare all surfaces and let them dry. Sand surfaces with 150-grit sandpaper and wipe with a tack cloth to remove any dust and sanding grit (top). Mask off all adjacent surfaces. Begin by painting the face frames, using a short foam roller (center).

Paint the insides of the doors and the drawer fronts (bottom). When the door backs are dry, paint the fronts. Depending on the paint you use, you may not need additional coats. If you do, allow the first coat of paint to dry overnight and sand all surfaces with 220-grit wet/dry sandpaper. Wipe with a tack cloth and apply the next coat. Once the painted surfaces are dry, install the drawers and attach the doors and handles.

painting trim

New wood trim can be painted ahead of time and then touched up once it's installed, or it can be painted in place, as with existing trim. If you are painting woodwork in place, always mask adjacent surfaces. When you apply two coats of semigloss or gloss paint to your trim, as is often the case, ensure a good bond by sanding lightly between coats and wiping the dust off with a tack cloth.

Begin with the mouldings closest to the ceiling and work down. You can paint your door and window trim and frames, as well as any cabinets, either before or after you complete the baseboards.

For the best results, paint narrower trim with a 1½-inch angled sash brush and use a 2-inch trim brush for wider trim. Begin about 3 inches from a corner and brush toward the corner, then brush in the opposite direction to spread the paint evenly (top). Start the next section several inches beyond where you stopped and paint back into the wet edge (center). Paint over any visible caulking.

A flexible edge guide is a handy tool for painting the baseboard below the carpet line. If you have a very tall baseboard with a wide flat surface topped with a moulded trim, first paint the moulded edge with an angled sash brush and then paint the wide surface with a wider brush.

pouncing

In this technique, you bounce the brush lightly up and down on a surface to create a dappled, translucent effect. It is used for several decorative painting effects, including stenciling.

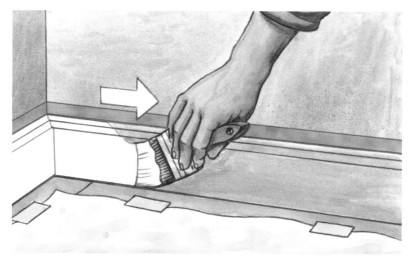

SPREAD PAINT EVENLY

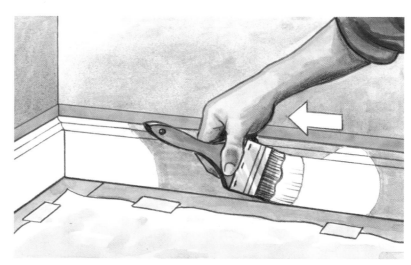

PAINT BACK INTO WET EDGE

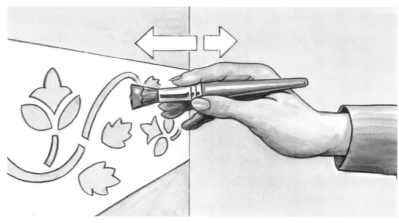

BOUNCE BRUSH AGAINST WALL

the final stage

AFTER YOU FINISH A PAINTING PROJECT, IT MAY BE TEMPTING TO THROW YOUR tools and materials aside and go take a nap. But the job is not complete until you clean up the work area and equipment, store your tools and paint, and dispose of rags and other waste appropriately.

cleaning up

Cleaning your tools and work area not only keeps your equipment in top shape but protects the environment from potential safety hazards. It's also much easier to clean up before paint dries.

If you plan to return to the project shortly, you can keep wet brushes and rollers wrapped tightly in plastic bags for several days. Put those used with alkyd paint in the freezer and those used with latex paint in the refrigerator.

Tools used with latex paint wash easily with soap and water. Use paint thinner to clean tools used with alkyd paint, and protect your hands with rubber gloves. Since you can't pour thinner down the drain, it's best to save used thinner in an old paint can, or any other container that won't be dissolved by the chemicals in the thinner, until you accumulate enough to dispose of it properly. Do not pour used thinner back into the original container. Thinner can be reused several times before it develops an unpleasant odor and is no longer effective.

cleaning brushes

Remove excess paint from brushes before washing them, instead of letting it go down the drain. You can do this in various ways. Brush the paint out on cardboard, put the brush between sheets of newspaper and press down as you pull out the brush, or use a special brush comb.

To clean remaining latex paint from a synthetic brush, hold the brush under running water until the water runs clear. Wash the brush with detergent and lukewarm water, forcing water into the bristles and the end of the ferrule. Rinse well.

To clean remaining alkyd paint from a brush, work paint thinner into the bristles. Then use a wire comb or brush to get

Right: Use paint thinner to clean alkyd paint from a brush, then blot with paper towels.

Far right: A bristle comb is especially good at removing paint from the bristles at the ferrule.

Opposite page: Scrape excess paint off a roller with a curved painter's tool.

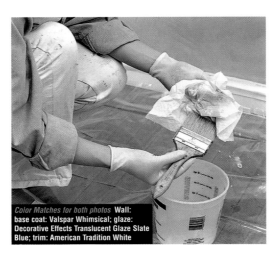

Color Matches for both photos **Wall: base coat: Valspar Whimsical; glaze: Decorative Effects Translucent Glaze Slate Blue; trim: American Tradition White**

out more paint. Once the brush is clean, remove excess thinner by blotting with paper towels, shaking the brush vigorously, lightly tapping the handle against a hard edge, or using a brush spinner designed to expel liquid from brushes. Wash the brush with warm water and bar soap; blot again. Clean up thinner with rags or paper towels. Be sure to dispose of them properly (see page 100).

After cleaning any brush, straighten the bristles with a bristle comb.

cleaning rollers and pad applicators

You may find it easier to dispose of roller covers and pads than to clean them, especially since they're relatively inexpensive. Those with cardboard tubes won't survive the cleaning anyway. (Be sure to dispose of them safely and according to local ordinances.) If you want to reuse covers or pads, squeeze out paint by pressing the roller or applicator against the bucket lip or the roller tray, or use a curved painter's tool to scrape the cover or pad dry. Scrape off any caked-on paint with a putty knife. Then remove the cover or pad.

Color Matches (American Tradition colors) Wall: Orchid Pearl; trim: White

Both covers and pads can be washed in the same way as brushes, using detergent and warm water for latex paint and paint thinner for alkyd paints. Once they're clean, squeeze out any excess liquid and blot lightly with a clean, absorbent cloth. Let the nap or pad dry completely. Wash the frames separately in the appropriate liquid.

cleaning yourself

Wet or dry latex paint readily washes off skin. However, latex that has dried doesn't wash off clothing, so be sure to launder clothes promptly.

A mechanic's hand cleaner will remove alkyd paint. It's easier on your skin than paint thinner and just as effective. Use the hand cleaner—not thinner—on fresh alkyd paint on clothing, then launder the items immediately.

storing brushes and paint

Once your paintbrushes are dry, wrap them in their original covers or in stiff paper. Store the brushes flat or hang them by their handles to maintain the proper shape of the bristles. Clean roller covers and applicator pads can be stored in plastic bags. Place roller covers on end to allow any water or paint thinner to drain and to prevent the nap from becoming flattened.

Leftover paint and thinner need to be stored safely. Most paint can be stored in a tightly closed can for several months or more. If less than a quarter of the paint remains in the can, transfer it to a smaller container where it's less likely to dry out. Before closing the lid, use a paper towel to clean out any paint from the groove. With a paper towel or rag over the lid, firmly hammer it on—without a tight seal, air can pass into the can and cause a skin to form on the top of the paint. Even with a tight seal, alkyd paint may still form a film, so place a piece of wax paper directly on top of the paint before you seal the can. Make sure you've labeled all cans with date, type of paint, color, and room where you used it.

Paint should never be stored outdoors or in an uninsulated shed or garage where temperatures go below freezing or above 100 degrees. Cold can cause paint to become lumpy and separate, and extreme heat can cause it to combust. Store paint thinner and flammable paints in a metal cabinet. Keep all paint products away from children and sources of flame or heat.

disposing of paint and rags

Because paint not easy to dispose of, you should plan your painting job carefully, buying only the amount of paint you're sure you can use, plus a little extra for touchups. If you end up with excess paint you don't want to store, offer it to a friend, a local shelter, or a theater company for painting sets. If you can't use or give it away, check the laws and guidelines in your community for the correct way to dispose of it. Some communities have particular days when they will accept paint and other hazardous materials for disposal. Others have scheduled days for picking up household hazardous waste, or special drop-off locations.

Here are some tips for dealing with particular materials.

latex paint

If a can of latex paint is almost empty, you can leave the can open and allow the paint to dry out in a well-ventilated area out of reach of children and animals. If you have larger quantities of paint, use a nontoxic paint hardener, which will shorten the drying process to a matter of minutes. (These water-absorbing crystals are also effective on spilled latex or acrylic paint.) Some communities will allow you to dispose of dried latex paint with your household trash; others won't, so check on proper disposal.

alkyd paint

A small amount of alkyd or other oil-base paint left in the bottom of a container can be mixed with some absorbent material such as cat litter and left to dry out in a well-ventilated area away from children, pets, and any source of spark or fire. When it's dry, seal the container tightly, label it, and dispose of it according to local ordinances.

rags and other materials

If you used rags, sponges, roller covers, foam brushes, or paper towels to work with or clean up oil-base or alkyd paint, paint thinner, or any other flammable liquid, be very careful how you handle them. When exposed to air, the flammable material can heat up and catch fire without a spark, a process that is called spontaneous combustion. Rags that are bunched or wadded up and thrown aside are especially prone to trap the heat as it develops and then burst into flames.

The best way to dispose of these materials is to spread them out to dry in a well-ventilated area away from children, pets, and any source of fire. Do not leave them unattended overnight. When they are dry, dispose of the materials according to local ordinances.

touchups

From time to time, it's necessary to touch up areas of your walls or ceilings that have nicks, scratches, or marks that can't be washed clean. If, as you finish a project, you notice a problem, wait until the paint has dried completely before touching it. If your paint job is older, thoroughly clean the surface and let it dry before applying new paint.

It is a good idea to keep a well-sealed can of the original paint on hand for these touchups. Ideally, you should also use the same applicator for your touchups as was used to apply the paint originally. If you brushed it on, for example, use a similar brush to add a dab of paint to the affected area. Use a dry brush loaded with a minimal amount of paint, and feather it out in all directions around the area you are touching up. You may have to thin the paint to reduce brush marks. If you rolled it, use a short roller with the same nap, also minimally loaded, to blend the new paint into the old. If you don't know what tool was used originally, you may have to do a little experimenting. If the first touchup creates a different texture, let it dry, sand it down, and try another applicator.

It's possible that a touched-up area will appear darker than the original coat. In this case, dilute your paint slightly—add water to latex paint or mineral spirits to alkyd paint—before you apply it. You may have to experiment with the dilution to get just the right tone.

If you don't have any of the original paint on hand, it may be difficult to match the color, unless you have the original paint chip or a piece of the painted material that can be computer color-matched. Even if you do have the old paint, it may not match: Natural light can fade the color. You may need to repaint the whole wall or ceiling for consistent color.

HOW TO REMOVE SPILLED PAINT

Accidents happen. If you prepared your area properly, putting down the necessary drop cloths, spilled paint should not be cause for replacing flooring or furniture. For paint that does hit an uncovered floor, sofa, or other target, here are some techniques that may—perhaps—save the day.

The key to removing spilled paint successfully is to clean it up immediately, while the paint is still wet. Once paint is dry it will be difficult, if not impossible, to remove completely.

Wet latex paint on wood, tile, or fabric can be wiped up with rags or paper towels. In the case of tile, be careful not to wipe paint into the grout lines as you clean it up. Any residue can be washed off with detergent and warm water. If you've spilled a significant amount of paint on a carpet or upholstery, use a putty knife or spatula to scrape up as much as you can. Then use a sponge dampened—not soaked—in warm soapy water to dab at the spill, working from the outside in. The paint should begin to dissolve quickly, but if it doesn't, give the water a few minutes to soak in. As the paint dissolves, blot up the liquid with paper towels. Don't rub at the spot and don't saturate it with more water or the stain may spread.

Dried latex paint can sometimes be removed from fabric by blotting the spot with a little alcohol on a rag. If that doesn't work, try a product called Goof Off, which is designed to remove latex coatings (it's available at Lowe's). Dried latex paint on tile or finished wood floors can be scraped off or removed with Goof Off.

Alkyd paint and other oil-base finishes are harder to remove. Alkyd paint spilled on fabric or carpeting should be scraped off immediately. Then dampen a rag with a solvent—mineral spirits, a dry cleaning solution, or nonbleaching Goof Off products such as Goo Remover or Hand Cleaner—and dab the spot as described for latex paint. If you use a solvent, be careful not to use too much or it will bleach the fabric. As the paint begins to dissolve into the solvent, blot it up with a dry rag or paper towels. Then use soapy warm water to rinse the area clean. Always follow appropriate safety precautions when handling solvents.

To remove wet alkyd paint from a ceramic floor, mop up the wet paint with a rag dampened in mineral spirits and wash away the residue with a heavy-duty degreaser. On a wood floor, mop up as much of the paint as you can and then use Goo Remover. Remove dried alkyd paint with lacquer thinner. Stronger solvents are too abrasive, and may remove the finish from sealed ceramic or finished wood floors.

simple paint projects

HOW OFTEN HAVE YOU THOUGHT, "I'D LOVE TO GIVE MY house a face-lift, but I don't have time"? The idea of taking on the whole house can be overwhelming—enough to keep you from ever getting started. But if you tackle small projects one room at a time, you'll be surprised at how quickly you can begin to transform your home.

Simple changes can yield dramatic results, as the following pages prove. This chapter includes 22 quick color projects. Most can be completed in a day and require minimal painting experience and no special artistic talent. Paint a single wall a stunning color or add stripes to your walls or floor. Stamp or stencil artful designs around the room or transform dull moulding with a fresh color. Give new life to furniture and accessories, coloring wood chairs in bright hues or applying a crackle finish to a magazine rack.

Once you get started, you might not want to stop, as each space becomes more inviting and you develop confidence in your painting abilities. For basic techniques for applying paint to walls, ceilings, or trim with brushes or rollers, see pages 88–97. Wear latex gloves for any project that includes oil-base products.

Color Matches on photos, designating paints available at Lowe's, have been provided by Valspar. Due to the limitations of the printing process, colors printed on the pages of this (or any) book may not be an exact representation of a specified paint or specialty product. Check paint chips at Lowe's for the true colors. If you like the color on the page better than the one on the paint chip, a Lowe's Paint Sales Specialist can mix a match for you.

quick changes with color

painting a single wall

FOR A FAST WAY TO ADD PIZZAZZ TO a tired-looking room, change the color of just one wall. If the room's current wall color is white, your color choices are almost limitless, dictated only by personal taste. Otherwise, select a color that either harmonizes with the current color or provides a stunning contrast. Look back at "All About Color," pages 8–39, to find inspiration for creating color schemes. Just remember that warm colors will add more energy to the room than cool ones.

If you have the time and energy, you don't have to limit yourself to just one wall. Paint each one a different color using either a split complementary or an analogous scheme (see pages 18–20). See pages 80–93 for instructions on how to prepare and paint a wall using a brush and roller.

If you prefer to paint one wall with a more decorative colorwashing technique, see pages 140–144.

In an open floor plan, painting a single wall a warm dark red gives this dining area definition and a sense of intimacy.

TOOLS AND MATERIALS

☐ Painter's masking tape	☐ 3-inch synthetic bristle brush
☐ Latex paint, satin	☐ Roller
☐ Paint bucket with grid	

Color Matches Accent wall: Eddie Bauer Home Cranberry; other walls and trim: American Tradition Linen White

painting chairs

AN EASY WAY TO REVITALIZE YOUR living space without having to clear out a room or tape walls is to paint furniture in bright colors. In this project we show you how to turn unfinished wood chairs into eye-catching centerpieces. Paint a set of chairs complementary colors (see page 19), or use the same color for all of them. Before you start on a chair, lay down a drop cloth or newspapers to protect the surface below.

TOOLS AND MATERIALS

- Unfinished wood chair(s)
- Sandpaper (100- to 120-grit)
- Tack cloth
- Wood primer
- Paint tray with liners
- 2-inch trim brush
- Painter's masking tape
- Enamel paint (1 quart per chair)
- Water-base polyurethane varnish, clear gloss

Color Matches **Wall: Laura Ashley Home Deep Cowslip 2; trim: American Tradition Ultra White; chair (American Tradition colors): Canary Yellow and Polished Apple**

A combination of bright red and yellow is a cheery coating for a wood chair. For more of a country look, use a soft slate blue paint (this is Olympic's Stormy Ridge).

1 Sand all of each chair to prevent rough spots that can show through paint. Wipe with a tack cloth to remove all dust.

2 Seal the wood with primer using a 2-inch trim brush.

3 Apply three coats of enamel paint, allowing each coat to dry completely before applying the next. If you are painting the chairs more than one color, always mask the areas you are not painting.

4 With a quart of enamel paint per chair, there will be some left over. Add ½ cup of clear gloss water-base polyurethane varnish to the remaining paint and apply a fourth coat. Let the final coat dry completely before you touch the chairs.

LOWE'S SAFETY TIP

Whenever you sand, make sure to wear a dust mask and protective glasses to keep the dust out of your mouth, nose, and eyes.

A red backdrop draws attention to a collection of dishware, while neutral black trim frames the display areas (see "Outlining a Room," opposite page).

Color Matches (American Tradition colors) Cabinet exterior: Filoli Morning Glory; cabinet interior: Cherokee Red; trim: Jack Black

PROJECT

highlighting a cabinet **interior**

PAINT COLORS CAN ADD APPEAL TO the interior of any cabinet. You might select a color that contrasts with the dominant color in your collection, such as a strong blue behind a set of yellow mugs. Or pick a color from your china pattern, such as the green of the leaves in a floral design. You can add to the project by painting the face trim of the cabinet; use either the same color as the adjacent walls or a contrasting color, depending on the effect you want to achieve.

TOOLS AND MATERIALS

- Painter's masking tape
- Wood primer
- Paint tray with liners
- 3-inch paintbrush or miniroller
- Latex paint, semigloss

LOWE'S QUICK TIP

Remember that a warm color such as red will bring the back of a cabinet forward. A cool color, on the other hand, will make a cabinet appear deeper.

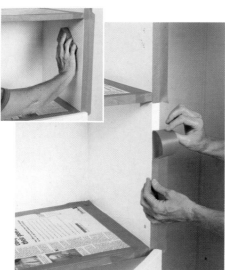

1 Mask the face edge or trim. Clean the inside of the cabinet. If you are painting a lighter color over an existing darker color, prime the surface.

2 Using a paintbrush or roller, paint the inside of the cabinet with semigloss latex paint. This is Olympic's Brass Mesh.

3 If necessary, apply a second coat of paint. Remove the tape and let the paint dry completely.

changing **trim** colors

Color Match **Wall: Earth Elements Earthen Red**

Instead of painting your walls, consider adding color to your trim, including crown moulding, baseboard, and door and window casings. The options here are almost endless. You can paint your trim in a single color to contrast or blend with your walls, or highlight the separate curves and grooves within a carved or stamped moulding in multiple colors for a more ornate effect. You can sponge paint onto the trim to give it visual texture (see pages 155–157), or stencil a design along it (see pages 118–125). You can also run a wallpaper border or painted design above or below a piece of trim to add more pattern to your room. Alternatively, you can make a light-colored room seem larger by "painting out" the trim—using the same hue as the wall color or a very close variant. Finally, if the colors of your walls change from room to room, you can use a single hue on trim throughout the house to make the overall color scheme more harmonious. See page 97 for instructions on painting trim.

TOOLS AND MATERIALS

- Painter's masking tape
- Latex or alkyd paint, semigloss
- Paint tray with liners
- 2-inch trim brush
- Angled sash brush

Above: Faux wood graining gives a new door and moulding old-fashioned character. A red line bordering the raised panels adds a contemporary twist to the treatment. See pages 198–205 for wood-graining projects.

Right: A multicolored scheme highlights the details of these mouldings, while the hues— soft leaf green and pale terra-cotta against cream-colored walls—create a restful ambience.

Color Matches (American Tradition colors) **Wall: Filoli Gold Ecru; trim: Verona Gold and La Fonda Sombrero**

OUTLINING A ROOM

Paint provides an easy way to outline a room's features, one that is less expensive than installing wood trim or wallpaper. For instance, consider painting a 3-inch-wide color border around a window opening. Create "crown mouldings" with a wide horizontal stripe of color along the top of the wall. You can add detail to it by notching or scalloping the bottom edge.

Or stamp a border of stars along the top of the wall instead. Stencil a leaf pattern around a doorway to replicate an arbor. Create the illusion of a country-style wainscot by painting the dado (the bottom third) of a wall in white, the upper portion in a soft pastel, and a 3-inch horizontal border between the two in a darker value of the pastel.

color's transforming power

WHILE WHITES AND NEUTRALS REMAIN A COMMON CHOICE FOR INTERIOR color schemes, sometimes a more vivid color can change the atmosphere and apparent size of a room to make it more appealing. The next several projects are designed to help you cope with problem areas in your home and convert seldom used spaces into ones you don't want to leave.

PROJECT

altering a room's **mood**

TOOLS AND MATERIALS

- Painter's masking tape
- Latex paint, satin
- Paint bucket with grid
- 3-inch synthetic bristle brush
- Roller

If your house has a large or open space that always feels cold and uninviting, paint it a warm color and you may find it transformed into your favorite room. Dark reds, terra-cottas, apricots, golden yellows, and even yellow-greens appear to advance and will make the room feel cozier, while at the same time giving it new energy.

The cooler colors—blue, green, and violet—are serene hues that seem to recede. A small room painted one of these colors appears more spacious than it really is.

The intensity and value of color (see page 10) also affect perceptions of the room. Intense or darker colors absorb light and make the room seem smaller and more intimate. Lighter values reflect light and open up the space, while low-intensity colors are calming and relaxing.

Right: A small living room becomes bright and airy with pale yellow walls and white trim.

Below: Brilliant red walls and ceiling add elegance and vibrancy to what was once an uninviting entry.

Color Matches Walls: Eddie Bauer Home Ochre; ceiling and trim: American Tradition Ultra White

Color Matches Walls: Waverly Home Classics Richly Red; trim: American Tradition Ultra White

reshaping a room

Choosing different colors for different walls in a room not only adds visual interest, but can alter the apparent proportions of the room. In a long, narrow room, you can paint an end wall a warm color, such as a deep ochre, and leave the side walls neutral or a very light value of that same color. This will draw the end wall in, giving the space a more pleasing proportion. In a square room, you can diminish the boxy look by painting two adjoining walls in contrasting colors; for example, pair peach with violet. Another way to create the same effect is to paint two facing walls a deeper tone of the color used on the other two walls. You can also enlarge any space by painting two adjoining walls with different colors that are analogous, such as marine blue and teal blue.

If you use more than one color on adjacent walls, make sure that the room's trim color works with all the wall colors. The trim can be the same color as one of the walls, a new color, or a neutral, such as white.

Color Matches **Left wall: Laura Ashley Home Cowslip 3; right wall: American Tradition Firebush**

Color Matches **(Alexander Julian at Home colors) Left wall: Copper Tone; right wall: Quartz**

Above: Two warm colors pull a broad corner together, making the walls seem closer and creating a dynamic space for entertaining.

Left: Two different values of neutral colors open up a tight corner.

LOWE'S QUICK TIP

When you are going to use different colors on adjoining walls, do a brush-out in the corner to test color combinations. See page 78 for more information on brush-outs.

TOOLS AND MATERIALS

- Painter's masking tape
- Latex paint, satin
- Paint bucket with grid
- 3-inch synthetic bristle brush
- Roller

altering the height of a ceiling

IN SOME HOMES, HIGH CEILINGS SEEM TO SOAR OUT OF SIGHT, MAKING THE room feel intimidating. Conversely, low ceilings in a large room can seem oppressive. Rather than planning expensive or impractical structural changes, try using color or pattern to alter the effect of height.

PROJECT

lowering a high ceiling

Color Matches (American Tradition colors) Walls: Rococo Yellow mixed into Decorative Effects Tintable Glaze; ceiling: Antique White; border: Nutmeg, Great Outdoors, Harper's Ferry, and Antique White

An easy way to make a tall ceiling feel lower is to paint it a darker shade than the walls. Another approach is to paint a crown moulding or the top 10 to 12 inches of the wall the same color as the ceiling. The eye rests on the lowest point of color, making the ceiling seem lower. To enhance the effect further, run a picture rail or other decorative moulding along the wall just below this section and paint it the same color as the ceiling and the upper wall. A stamped, stenciled, or wallpaper border, either at the top of the wall or several inches below the ceiling, can also reduce the sense of height.

To stencil or stamp a pattern border, see pages 118–129. If you want to hang a wallpaper border, use the Wallpaper Calculator at www.lowes.com to estimate how much you need. A Lowe's Wallpaper Sales Specialist can verify your calculations and answer your questions. Also ask about how-to booklets and clinics offered at Lowe's.

TOOLS AND MATERIALS

- Painter's masking tape
- Latex paint, satin
- Paint tray with liners
- 3-inch synthetic bristle brush
- Roller

Using warm colors from the Swedish wall sconce, a hand-painted border with faux-rope swags pulls the eye down from this 11-foot-high ceiling. The delicate background wall texture was achieved by applying a translucent golden glaze with a large sponge covered in cheesecloth (see pages 155–157 for sponging instructions).

Color Matches (American Tradition colors) Wall and crown moulding: Gold Stock; trim and ceiling: Dover White; stencils: Light Lime, Hint of Lime, and Dark Leather; wall in room to right: Filoli Gold Ecru; ceiling in room to right: Light Lime

A ceiling trimmed with crown moulding seems higher when the ceiling is painted white and the trim is the same color as the wall. Leaves stenciled in a vertical pattern also increase the sense of height.

PROJECT

raising a low ceiling

When a ceiling feels too low, paint both the walls and ceiling light colors, with the ceiling lighter than the walls. White is a good color for low ceilings, but light values of cool colors also give a sense of height because they seem to recede. Another good trick is to use shading on the wall, starting with a lighter color at the ceiling and darkening it as you move toward the floor. Always paint the ceiling before the walls.

TOOLS AND MATERIALS

- Painter's masking tape
- Latex paint, satin
- Paint tray with liners
- 3-inch synthetic bristle brush
- Roller

LOWE'S QUICK TIP

To paint ceilings, put your roller on a telescoping extension pole, preferably one with a range of 4 to 8 feet. This will allow you to paint without a stepladder and to work to the side of the area you're painting so you won't get splattered.

Painted to imitate a circus tent, this bedroom provides a fun atmosphere for any child. On the ceiling, stripes—yellow glaze applied with a brush—give the illusion of a canopy. The artist added a shadow on one side of each stripe and softened the other edge to enhance the appearance of draped fabric. A faux rope appears to hold the canopy in place, and a painted border at the top of the wall mimics the fabric valance hanging over the bed. The room displays the professional skills of the decorative artist who created it, but do-it-yourselfers can easily paint the wall stripes, as shown here.

Color Matches (American Tradition colors) Walls, ceiling, and trim: White Essence, Southern Beauty Red, and Country Club Green; stripes: Chadwyck Yellow mixed into Decorative Effects Tintable Glaze

PROJECT

striping a wall for added height

Vertical stripes visually heighten and narrow the surface to which they are applied by moving the observer's eye up the wall. Stripes can have identical widths, different widths, or run in a pattern—perhaps one or two narrow lines separated by wider stripes in a contrasting color. For a more subtle effect, use the same color of paint with different sheens, such as a glossy stripe next to a matte one; in that case, apply the matte finish first. Or, consider using a decorative painting technique on one of the stripe colors, such as spattering, dragging, or ragging (see pages 148–151 and 158–161).

TOOLS AND MATERIALS

Painter's masking tape	Tape measure
Latex paint, satin	Plumb bob
Paint tray with liners	Chalk line
Roller	Paintbrush or narrow roller

1 Mask any areas you are not painting. Cover the wall in the base color (the lightest color stripe—here, Olympic's Spiced Vinegar). Remove the tape and let the paint dry completely.

2 Carefully measure the width you plan for each stripe and the distance between them. Professionals suggest stripes that are 3 to 5 inches wide. Use a plumb bob to establish perfectly vertical lines for the edges of your stripes. Mark points along these lines at the top and bottom of the wall. Snap chalk lines on the marks.

3 Mask the ceiling and walls adjacent to the starting wall, and mask the baseboard. Apply tape along the outside edges of each stripe to be painted and tape an X across the areas that will retain the base color. After taping, wipe off chalk lines with a clean paper towel.

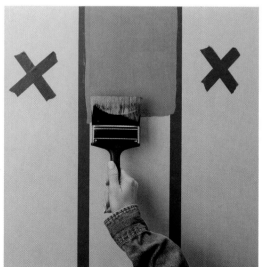

4 Paint the stripe areas not marked with an X, working in short, vertical strokes with a brush or narrow roller. The color here is Olympic's Allspice. Promptly remove the tape before the paint dries. If paint has seeped under the tape, use a touchup brush to clean up the lines.

LOWE'S QUICK TIP
Many chalk lines come with blue chalk that is difficult to wipe off. You can empty out the chalk compartment and refill it with a mixture of 3 parts talcum powder to 1 part blue chalk.

hiding and highlighting

PAINT ALSO PROVIDES A QUICK FIX FOR DETAILS THAT ARE UNSIGHTLY OR JUST undistinguished—an old-fashioned heat register, flat hollow-core doors that add nothing to your decor, or bland or unattractive trim. You can use paint to make these features virtually disappear—or to transform them into decorative focal points.

PROJECT

camouflaging unwanted elements

Unless your interior style is eclectic or very creative, you probably prefer to hide details you wish weren't there, rather than call attention to them. The best way to do that is to have them blend in with their backgrounds. Anything painted the same color as the walls will tend to disappear. For features made of metal, especially metal that contains iron, first remove any rust or oxidation, then apply an acrylic latex or alkyd corrosion-resistant primer.

TOOLS AND MATERIALS

- Painter's masking tape
- Corrosion-resistant primer (for metal)
- Latex paint, satin
- Paint tray with liners
- Synthetic bristle brush
- Roller

Color Matches (American Tradition colors) Door and wall: Garnet Glory; cabinets: Ultra White

Below: A 1950's scallop trim almost disappears when it's painted the same color as the walls and ceiling—an inexpensive approach to a detail that doesn't go with your decor.

Color Match American Tradition White

Left: Painted the same dark color as the wall and casing, a poorly placed closet door becomes part of the background, while new white cabinetry draws attention.

This cabinet door acquired a new role as a message board. To make an asset of a door, recessed panel, or wall this way, paint it with two coats of blackboard paint, a scrubbable matte-finish paint available at Lowe's.

Color Matches Walls and cabinets: American Tradition Ultra White; right wall: American Tradition Garnet Glory

PROJECT

perking up dull **details**

Sometimes dull features can be turned into unexpected focal points that add character to a room. Sponging a flat door or flat casings gives them texture and a new life without any other modifications (see pages 155–157). If you are using lots of color on your walls, painting a feature-less door or trim a contrasting color can add excitement to the room.

Baseboard heaters or steam heat registers may not be particularly attractive in and of themselves, but by adding a little pattern—stripes, spots, clouds, flowers—you can make them interesting touches rather than eyesores. Match colors or patterns to upholstery or other surfaces in the room to create an integrated design scheme.

TOOLS AND MATERIALS

- Painter's masking tape
- Latex paint, satin
- Paint tray with liners
- Synthetic bristle brush
- Roller

combining color with pattern

A SIMPLE WAY TO ENLIVEN YOUR WALLS WITHOUT COMPLETELY REPAINTING them is to add a touch of pattern. There are several ways to do this with paint, including rolling, stenciling, and stamping. For a more extensive pattern, try wallpapering.

rolling on **pattern**

One of the easiest and least expensive ways to add pattern to a wall is to roll it on. With just a roller, masking tape, and paint, you can create a pattern of squares all over a wall or a "wainscot" on its lower portion, as in the two projects that follow. You can also use this method to roll horizontal stripes across a wall.

This simple technique employs tape on 9-inch rollers. Different widths of tape change the dimensions of the squares or the wainscot stripes. You can create exact spacing by wrapping one piece of tape loosely around the end of the roller, then wrapping the adjacent section as tightly as possible. Repeat this process until you get to the end of the roller, then remove the loose tape before painting.

PROJECT

rolling on **minisquares**

Color Matches (American Tradition colors) Wall: base coat: White Sand; pattern: Ultra White

TOOLS AND MATERIALS

Painter's masking tape	1-inch masking tape
Latex paint, satin, 2 colors (or 1 color in 2 sheens)	2-foot level
	Plumb bob
Paint tray with liners	Water-soluble lead pencil
Roller with at least 2 covers	Paintbrush

1 Tape off any areas you do not wish to paint. Apply the base coat in the color you want the squares to be. Remove the tape and let the paint dry completely. Starting 1 inch from one end of a roller cover, apply bands of masking tape so that every other inch on the roller is covered (you'll end up with four taped sections and five untaped).

A white-on-gray pattern adds subtle yet dynamic visual character to a room. This treatment looks best when you use two values of the same color or two similar colors.

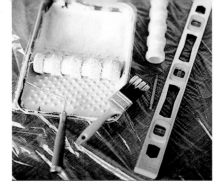

2 Set a level vertically against the end of the wall, at the bottom. Using its width, mark a guideline from the floor to the ceiling, checking to be sure it is straight and plumb with a plumb bob. Load your roller with the second color, place it against the line you just marked, and roll from top to bottom of the wall without stopping. Repeat across the wall, always overlapping one previously painted line to maintain even spacing. Roll as far down as you can without touching the floor with the roller. Check periodically to make sure your stripes are plumb; mark new guidelines if necessary.

3 When you've finished the vertical lines, let them dry. Then use the width of the level to mark a horizontal guideline near the floor from one side of the wall to the other. (The line should be level, even though your floor will probably have high and low spots.) Paint the horizontal lines in the same fashion you did the vertical ones, rolling from one side of the wall to the other without stopping. When the horizontal lines are dry, use the level to mark a line near the floor and paint a false baseboard in either color with a paintbrush. Use the paintbrush to touch up the lines if necessary.

rolling on a **wainscot**

Painted-on wainscoting and door trim make up a contemporary version of traditional design elements. Rolled-on pattern works best over untextured walls.

TOOLS AND MATERIALS

- Painter's masking tape
- Latex paint, 3 colors, satin
- Paint tray with liners
- Roller with at least 2 covers
- 2-foot level
- Water-soluble lead pencil
- Paintbrush
- 1½-inch masking tape

1 Tape off any areas you do not wish to paint. With a roller, apply the lightest of your three paint colors as the base coat over the whole wall. Remove the tape and let the paint dry completely. When it is dry, use the width of your level to mark a line around the top and sides of each doorway. Use a brush to paint this area in the darkest color to create the illusion of a door casing. Use the level to mark a line where the top of your faux wainscot will be—the general rule is either one third or two thirds of the distance between the floor and ceiling.

2 Starting 1½ inches from one end of a roller cover, divide its length into alternate bands of taped and untaped sections that are 1½ inches wide. Repeat on a second roller cover.

Color Matches **(American Tradition colors) Above chair rail: Bone White; stripes: Montpelier Madison White and Ultra White**

3 Using one of the wrapped roller covers and the darkest color of paint, place your roller so that it overlaps the painted door casing. Starting at the horizontal guideline you marked along the wall, roll toward the floor in one continuous motion. Repeat across the wall, always overlapping one previously painted stripe to maintain proper spacing. Using the remaining, medium-value color, position the other wrapped roller cover at one end of the wainscot so it will paint the gaps between the painted stripes. It's okay if the edges between the stripes are not precise. Continue across the wall. Use a brush to touch up the stripes if necessary. When the paint is dry, use the level to mark guidelines for a false baseboard and cornice moulding. Paint with the brush and the darkest paint color.

working with precut **stencils**

PRECUT STENCILS ARE AVAILABLE IN myriad patterns to suit every architectural style—traditional, contemporary, sophisticated, and whimsical. Although some stencils can be applied wherever you choose—on a cabinet door, on the back of a chair, all over the wall—others are designed to create a border. A single-color motif is easiest to apply because there is only one stencil. A multicolor one may have a stencil for every color and you must carefully superimpose each stencil over the portion of the design you have already painted, after the paint has dried.

This two-color stencil along the top of a bathroom wall is accompanied by stamped sea creatures in the same light green (American Tradition Green Stroll) and blue (American Tradition Woodlawn Blue Angel).

If you don't see a design you want to repeat around your room, consider combining several unrelated ones. Changing colors can also transform a simple stencil into one with unexpected visual appeal. For instance, use a stencil of a single rose but alternate pink, yellow, and peach as you work across the wall.

This project involves a two-color motif with two stencils. When working with more than one stencil, you use registration marks to position the second (and any following) stencil precisely. A registration mark may be a small circle or crossed lines cut in the corners of the stencil sheets; you apply paint in these cutouts to make a mark on the wall. Or the stencil may have a cutout of an element of the design already painted; you superimpose the new stencil over the dry paint. If you don't want visible registration marks on the wall, place small pieces of masking tape on the wall where the registration marks will hit. Remove the tape after stenciling.

You can simplify the project by using a single color—or make it more complex by adding a third color freehand after all your stenciling has dried. See pages 122–125 for stencil patterns you can copy.

TOOLS AND MATERIALS

Carpenter's level	Latex paint, satin;
Masking tape	or acrylic stencil
Precut stencil(s)	paint
Hobby knife	Mixing containers
Spray adhesive	Stencil brushes
with adjustable	Paper towels
spray tip	Small artist's
Latex gloves	brush

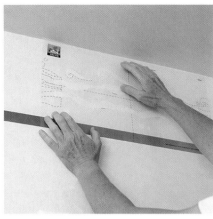

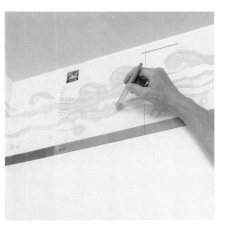

1 Using a carpenter's level, mark points for the bottom of the stenciled border. Press masking tape along the line. Use a hobby knife to clear away parts of the pattern that are not cut out completely. Pick a starting point and plan the stencil spacing. Especially with stencils that won't bend, try to have the design end before corners; acetate stencils can work around corners (see Step 4). Spray adhesive on the back of the stencil, adjusting the tip so the spray covers its width; let the adhesive set until it is tacky. Line up the stencil's lower edge with the tape guideline and press it into position.

2 Pour the first color into a container. If your stencil doesn't indicate color, write it on a masking tape label on the side of the stencil that will face you when you paint. Using a circular motion, swirl a stencil brush in the paint. Rub the bristles over a paper towel, so the brush is almost dry. Working from the outside of the stencil in, lightly pounce the brush into each cutout (see page 97). Do not brush sideways or paint may get under the stencil. Vary the angle of the brush to achieve texture; let some of the wall color show through. Make the paint as translucent, opaque, or varied as you like.

3 Remove the stencil carefully. Reposition it along the tape guideline, aligning its registration marks with those on the section just painted. Apply paint to the cutouts, reposition the stencil, and continue around the wall, cleaning the stencil with a rag or sponge and reapplying adhesive as needed. Complete the full length of the border with the first stencil before working with the second.

4 If you are turning a corner with an acetate stencil, match its registration marks with the pattern already painted and tape or stick that side of the stencil in place. Then gently press the stencil into the corner, bending but not creasing it, and tape or stick the other side in place. Apply paint to the cutouts, working as far into the corner as possible.

5 When you have finished applying the first color and the paint is completely dry, pour the second color into a container. Position the second stencil at the starting point, matching up the registration marks. Repeat steps 2 through 4, using a clean stencil brush.

6 Correct errors and fill in gaps after completing the entire border. Most stencils have bridges that hold the pattern together; you should fill in the gaps they leave. Use an artist's brush to fill in gaps or any missed cutouts. Work with an almost dry brush and pounce the surface lightly.

making **your own** stencils

WHILE YOU MAY FIND A READY-MADE STENCIL that is perfect for your home, making your own also has its advantages. Not only will it be unique, but it will give you the satisfaction of having created it. Making your own stencil also enables you to match a favorite decorative element in your home—you can reduce or enlarge it as necessary on a photocopying machine. See pages 122–125 for some stencil patterns you can use or adapt in cutting your own stencils.

The number of stencils required for a design depends on the number of colors involved and the intricacy of the design. While you can apply more than one color to a single stencil, it is easiest if you have a separate stencil for each color. The simplest designs are often the most effective and can be executed in the least time. The most convenient material for making stencils is clear acetate since its transparency allows you to layer a number of sheets and still see the design clearly. Stencil board is another possibility, but it won't allow you to see those additional layers.

TOOLS AND MATERIALS

▪ Technical drawing pen and ink	▪ Clear acetate (.0075 gauge)
▪ Graph paper	▪ Ruler
▪ Colored pencils or markers	▪ Hobby knife and supply of sharp blades
▪ Spray adhesive	

LOWE'S | SAFETY TIP
When cutting acetate, always have a hard cutting surface under the acetate and never place your hand in the path of the blade.

Right: Stencils don't have to run horizontally around a room or cover the walls. Here, a stenciled design set inside every other vertical stripe adds pattern to a neutral color scheme. This hand-cut stencil, inspired by the pattern in the Tibetan rug, is a light oyster against a ragged glaze (see pages 158–161 for instructions on ragging).

Far right: Stenciled stars and comets turn a plain blue chair into a personalized work of art. The stencil colors are Valspar's American Tradition Iceland Night and Green Stroll, applied over Olympic's Stormy Ridge.

Color Matches Walls: Earth Elements Something in the Air mixed into Decorative Effects Tintable Glaze; trim: American Tradition White Essence; stencil: Decorative Effects Translucent Pearl Glaze

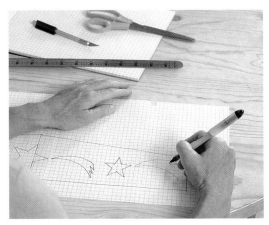

1 With a technical pen, draw a design to the desired size on graph paper, or photocopy a design out of a book in the exact size you need. If you're copying from a stencil book, the design will already have bridges, the narrow strips that separate the different parts of the design and stop the stencil from falling apart. (The larger the bridge, the easier it is to apply more than one color.) If necessary, insert bridges in logical places. Make clear photocopies of the design, one for each color in the design. On each copy, color the shapes that will be cut out for that stencil.

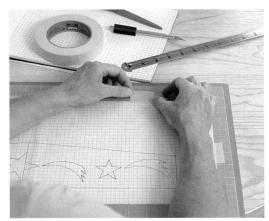

2 Coat the back of each photocopy with spray adhesive and press it firmly against a piece of the acetate to use as a cutting guide. Trim the acetate, leaving a 1-inch margin around the design. If you are creating a border stencil, make sure the bottom edge, which will sit on the tape guideline, is straight. Alternatively, if it is inconvenient for you to make photocopies, tape an acetate piece over the design and trace the areas that will be painted with the first color. If you're using more than one color, leave this acetate in place and tape successive pieces on top, one for each color.

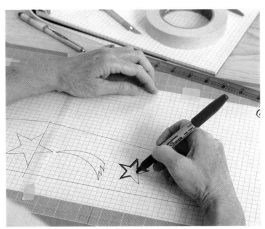

3 To make registration marks so you can align the separate acetates as you work, you have two options. You can place the stencils on top of each other so that the design is aligned and punch a small hole at each corner. Or on each stencil, trace a section (don't cut it out) of an element of the design, such as a leaf, that gets painted in your first stencil. When you place this second or third stencil on the wall to work, superimpose the tracing over that particular element. Mark the top front side of each acetate and number the stencils in the order they will be used.

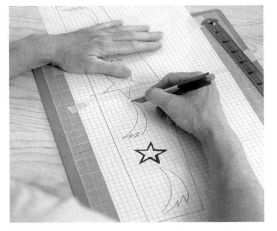

4 Place the acetates one at a time on a flat, firm cutting surface. Cut the stencil design with a hobby knife, drawing the blade slowly toward you in a smooth, continuous motion. When you're cutting curves, turn the design rather than the knife. Trim any jagged edges that remain after the original cut is made. Any imperfect edges won't be noticeable in the finished work. After each stencil is cut, remove the photocopy.

LOWE'S QUICK TIP

For ease in cutting curves and free-form shapes on acetate, use a wood-burning tool with a stencil-cutting tip, available at craft shops.

stencil **patterns**

THE STENCIL TEMPLATES ON THESE PAGES CAN BE DUPLICATED ON A COPIER IN any size that is appropriate for the application you have in mind. Borders can be created using one of the horizontal schemes or by putting one or more single motifs together in a repeating pattern. These patterns may also serve as inspiration for a design you make up on your own—instead of cherries, try apples or a watermelon slice. Or create more nautical motifs to accompany the sailboat. Refer to the previous two pages for directions on cutting out your own stencils. Apply the stencils as directed on pages 118–119.

stamping

Color Match **Walls: American Tradition Blue Willow**

Stamps can be applied in a controlled or random pattern, or a combination of the two, such as this playful arrangement of flowers across a wall. The stamp paint color is Olympic's Green Grapes.

TOOLS AND MATERIALS

- Latex paint, satin; or prepared glaze (½ pint for a 10- by 12-foot room)
- Containers for stamp colors
- Latex gloves
- 1-inch artist's brushes (one for each color)
- Stamps (one for each color)
- Cardboard
- Carpenter's level
- ¼-inch artist's brush

STAMPING, ONE OF THE OLDEST OF printing methods, has become one of the hottest trends in decoration today. It is easy to do and can be used on almost any surface and in any color. You can stamp a design randomly across a wall or confine it to a border around the room, as in the project shown here.

Stamps can be as sophisticated or as playful as your taste or needs dictate. The materials are equally varied. Stamps can be purchased in rubber or foam or can be made at home out of dense sponge or hard vegetables or fruits, such as potatoes, apples, or pears, that stay firm when cut. Foam stamps hold more paint than rubber ones and can give your design a sponge-like texture. Vegetable stamps will print the natural texture of the vegetable as long as

you don't cover their surface too heavily with paint. After cutting, remove seeds. Vegetable stamps hold paint in different ways; experiment before you commit to a design. See pages 128–129 for stamp patterns you can use.

The same stamp can produce different effects depending on the colors you use. If you plan to use more than one color, have a separate stamp for each color so the colors don't mix.

The color of your stamp should complement the wall color. For the most subtle effect, use the same color, or an analogous one, in a different paint finish than you've used on the wall, putting matte stamps on a semigloss wall, or vice versa. To make stamps stand out dramatically, use boldly contrasting colors.

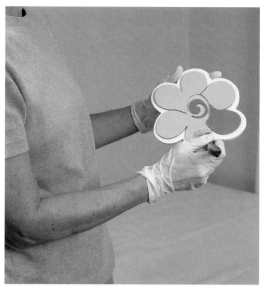

1 Pour about 4 ounces of paint into a container. If you are using more than one color of paint, you will need a separate container for each color. Put on latex gloves to work. Dip an artist's brush in a color and lightly apply the paint to one side of the stamp. Avoid putting too much paint on the stamp, since excess paint can collect in gaps and bleed into your design. Use a different brush for each stamp to prevent the colors from mixing.

2 Test the stamp on a sheet of cardboard to make sure it produces the look you desire. Use a large sheet of cardboard to experiment until you determine the most pleasing arrangement for your stamp. You might apply it randomly over your wall or on the diagonal; it can embellish a cabinet front, frame a window or door, or create a border. To stamp a border, mark a level line at a set distance below the ceiling. Draw a second line far enough below the first that the space between will accommodate your design.

3 Load the stamp with your first color and discharge excess paint on the cardboard. Beginning at one end of the wall, press the stamp evenly into the wall surface. Load the stamp with paint and blot away the excess each time you use it. If the stamped pattern is a bit uneven, you can use a 1/4-inch artist's brush to fill in any gaps.

LOWE'S QUICK TIP

To create your own stamp, you can purchase rubber stamp blocks in various sizes. Draw your design on a piece of paper and then transfer it onto the rubber using carbon paper. Carve away the areas that are not part of your design, leaving a raised area about 1/2 inch high. Always cut away from the design at an angle.

stamp patterns

CUT RUBBER, FOAM, SPONGE, OR EVEN VEGETABLES TO CREATE STAMPS USING the designs on these pages. Copy any design, such as a star, in various sizes or flip an irregular shape to give you a variety of similar shapes you can stamp randomly across a wall. For other motifs, look at the stencil designs on pages 122–125, some of which can be adapted for stamping. Other stamping ideas include geometric shapes (triangles, circles, squares for a checkerboard pattern), bugs and butterflies, and vegetables and fruits. A 4- by 8-inch rectangular stamp dipped in dark red will give you a great faux-brick pattern. To use the patterns shown here, copy on a photocopy machine, enlarging the design if you wish. Cut out the shape, lay it on the material you are using, and trace the shape, or use carbon paper to transfer it to the face of a rubber block (see tip, page 127). With a paring or hobby knife, cut out the shape. Follow the instructions on pages 126–127 to stamp your pattern.

A B C

1 2 3

striping a wood floor

IT WAS ONCE POPULAR TO ADD PATTERN to a floor with paint or stain, rather than rugs or carpeting. Today such methods as stenciling, trompe l'oeil, faux finishes, and stain applications that mimic inlay are being used on floors again. Some of these techniques require advanced skills, but simple geometric designs like the one in this striping project are easy to achieve. Alternating painted boards and boards with a clear finish emphasizes the wood grain, creating an interesting contrast to the applied color. Choose a tone to match or complement the room's furnishings. A latex interior paint is suitable if you follow up with a polyurethane finish over the entire floor. Or consider using a wood stain in a color that stands out from the natural wood, such as dark blue or green.

LOWE'S QUICK TIP

Whenever you are removing baseboard from the bottom of a wall, gently pull it off with a pry bar, protecting the wall behind it with a wood shim.

TOOLS AND MATERIALS

Pry bar	Latex paint, satin
Nail set	Paint tray with
Hammer	liners
Pole sander	4-inch roller
Waterproof sand-	Polyurethane
paper (80-grit)	finish, satin
Tack cloth	2-inch paintbrush
Tape measure	Pole finish
Low-tack masking	applicator
tape	Floor polisher with
Latex gloves	180-grit screen

1 Remove the quarter-round shoe moulding at the bottom of the baseboard to expose the flooring edges. (If you don't have shoe moulding, and there is no gap between the baseboard and floor, you may need to remove the baseboard.) Examine the flooring for protruding nails and sink the heads with a nail set and a hammer. Fit a pole sander with 80-grit waterproof sandpaper—regular sandpaper tends to clog up on finished surfaces. Wearing a dust mask and protective glasses, sand the entire floor in the direction of the wood grain, changing the sandpaper as necessary. Once the sanding is completed, vacuum thoroughly and wipe the flooring with a tack cloth.

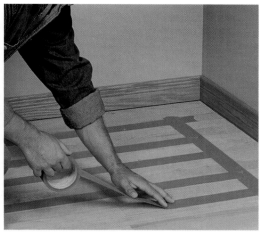

2 In this design, sets of two painted floorboards alternate with sets of three unpainted floorboards within an unpainted border at the perimeter that is equal to the width of three floorboards. To lay out the border, measure the width of three floorboards and mark that distance from the baseboard on the ends of the floorboards. Where the floorboards run parallel to the baseboard, simply count three boards out and make your mark.

3 With low-tack masking tape, mark off the outer edges of the border and the sets of floorboards to be painted. Press the tape down firmly along its entire length to ensure a good seal; overlap the ends. To avoid mistakes, mark an X on each area to be left unpainted.

Color Match for stripes **American Tradition Montpelier Olive**

4 Load a roller with paint and roll off the excess. Working in the direction of the wood grain, apply the paint to the floorboards. Start away from the taped edges, then work along them once the roller is no longer fully loaded, reducing the risk of bleeding under the tape. Roll directly along the edges of the tape to ensure crisp painted edges. Let the paint dry to the touch, then peel off the tape. (If you wait too long, the tape may lift paint along the edges.) Lightly sand any bleed marks (remember to wear a dust mask and protective glasses) and wipe away dust with a tack cloth.

5 When the paint is thoroughly dry, pour a quantity of clear finish into a paint tray. Cut in the edges of the flooring along the baseboards with a 2-inch paintbrush. Complete the rest of the flooring with a pole finish applicator; work in the direction of the wood grain. Allow the finish to dry for the time recommended by the manufacturer, then apply a second coat and let it dry. Wearing a dust mask and protective glasses, lightly sand the flooring using a floor polisher loaded with a 180-grit screen, then vacuum and wipe with a tack cloth. Make a final application of clear finish and let it dry for two or three days before reattaching the shoe moulding and moving furniture back into the room.

enhancing color with texture

SPECIALTY PAINTS OFFER EASY WAYS TO ADD TEXTURE TO YOUR WALLS OR accessories. With these products, you don't need any special talent other than the ability to use a roller and paintbrush, yet the end result can look like you've hired a professional.

PROJECT

creating a **grasscloth** effect

Walls covered in grasscloth add an informal sophistication to any room. By using a textured paint instead of actual cloth to create this effect, you eliminate the need for meticulous cutting and wallpapering with sticky glue. The effect can be produced in a wide range of colors. You can purchase the textured paint already tinted; you can also brush on colored glaze.

TOOLS AND MATERIALS

Painter's masking tape	Texture roller
Decorative Effects Sand Texture paint (Valspar)	Texture brush
	Color glaze
	Paintbrush
Paint tray with liners	Rag

The Sand Texture paint can be tinted to 19 different colors. Shown here is Amberlight, topped with Burnt Sienna and Buff color glazes.

1 Tape off any areas you do not wish to paint. Load a texture roller with the texture paint and apply it to the walls as you would standard latex paint (see pages 91–93).

2 Using a texture brush, start at the top corner of the wall and drag the brush from top to bottom in one continuous stroke to create vertical lines. Work from one end of the wall to the other, overlapping each vertical section by about 2 inches. Let paint dry. To add a glaze color, dip a paintbrush in the glaze and brush the glaze into the texture, using random strokes across the wall. Use a rag to blot excess glaze and soften the color as desired.

imitating brushed suede

A wall that appears covered in the velvety texture of brushed suede provides a sense of casual elegance. Suede specialty paints are suitable for wood, plaster, or wallboard, although they shouldn't be used on trim. Multiple layers of paint are vital with this finish, since each brushstroke adds depth and dimension. Random, irregular brush-strokes are the key to a successful finish.

TOOLS AND MATERIALS

- Painter's masking tape
- Decorative Effects Brushed Suede paint (Valspar)
- Paint tray with liners
- Roller with ½-inch nap
- 3- to 4-inch paintbrush

The suede effect on this wall is so persuasive, you almost need to touch it to believe it's only paint. The color is Sun Baked Clay.

1 Tape off any areas you do not wish to paint. Apply the first coat of paint using a roller. Work in 3-foot-square sections and finish each one before moving to the next. Once the entire surface is completed, roll from ceiling to floor in one direction to even out any lap marks. Remove the tape and allow the paint to dry for at least four hours before applying the second coat.

2 Reapply the tape, if necessary. For the second coat, load a 3- to 4-inch brush with paint and apply it to the wall in a series of overlapping 1-foot Xs.

3 Continue to apply paint across sur-face, using smaller, 4- to 6-inch Xs over the entire area to create subtle vari-ations in tone. Use both the broad and the narrow side of the brush as you work. Random strokes are essential. Remove the tape and allow the paint to dry.

This table has all the visual advantages of solid metal and stone, but is a fraction of the cost and the weight of the real thing.

giving a table a **rusted finish**

The look of stone and metal furniture is the ideal complement to a rustic-style home. But the real thing can be expensive as well as cumbersome to move around. You can get much the same effect by using specialty paints on unfinished wood pieces, such as the console table shown here. This example uses a combination of Decorative Effects paints from Valspar to replicate stone and rusted iron, but you can also use specialty paints to create finishes that convincingly mimic granite, weathered wood, or aged copper, among other options.

LOWE'S QUICK TIP

Always practice your technique on paper before starting your project.

TOOLS AND MATERIALS

- Unfinished wood table
- Sandpaper
- Tack cloth
- Painter's masking tape
- Copper Sky Base Coat (Valspar)
- Paint tray with liners
- 2-inch paintbrushes or minirollers
- Cotton cheesecloth
- Pewter metal glaze (Valspar)
- Natural sea sponges (large and small)
- Bucket filled with water
- Mocha translucent color glaze (Valspar)
- Olde Towne Base Coat (Valspar)
- Buff translucent color glaze (Valspar)

1 Wearing a dust mask and protective glasses, sand all the surfaces of the table smooth and clean off all dust with a tack cloth. Then, starting with the base, carefully tape off all areas to which you do not want to apply the special finish.

2 With a 2-inch paintbrush or a small roller, apply Copper Sky Base Coat to the legs and base. Remove the tape and allow the paint to dry overnight.

3 Reapply the tape and dip a wad of cheesecloth in some Pewter metal glaze. Randomly dab the glaze across the surface of the legs and base. A diagonal drifting of pattern will look more natural than a vertical or horizontal row. Keep in mind that this specialty glaze has a faster drying time than typical glazes.

4 Dampen a large sea sponge in a bucket of water and wring it out well. Dab it in some Mocha glaze, loading the sponge evenly. Lightly pounce the surface with the sponge, concentrating the color in areas around the glaze you applied in Step 3. To reach into tight spaces and corners, use a small damp sea sponge. Remove the tape and allow the glaze to dry overnight.

5 After the base is completely dry, turn the table upside down and tape off the base. Starting with the underside of the table and moving to the top, apply a base coat of Olde Towne paint with a small roller or brush. Remove the tape and allow the paint to dry overnight.

6 Reapply the masking tape and dip a paintbrush in Buff color glaze. Using an X pattern, cover the underside and top of the table in a random pattern until all the glaze is removed from the brush. While the glaze is still wet, dab it with a wad of cheesecloth to remove any brushstrokes and soften the look.

painting make-overs for everyday objects

CAREFULLY CHOSEN ACCENT PIECES CAN ADD INTEREST, PERSONALITY, TEXTURE, and color to a home. Use a special finish to bring new life to an outdated or worn-looking vase, pot, planter, box, candlestick, or picture frame. Depending on the manufacturer, you can find textured paints that duplicate stone, metal, or other finishes. These specialty spray paints can be used on wood, metal, ceramic, glass, plastic, or even rigid polystyrene foam to revitalize old accessories. Before you start, spread a drop cloth or newspapers under the item to protect the surface underneath it.

Using spray paint is no more difficult than any other kind of painting, but it does require some care. Practice first on a scrap piece of wood or cardboard, making sure to avoid excessive buildups that can produce visible runs. Hold the can upright about 8 to 10 inches from the surface and paint in smooth, continuous horizontal sprays, making sure to depress the contact only after the can is in motion. Release the contact as you approach the end of each line. Take special care in masking adjacent areas, always work in a well-ventilated area, and never spray paint outdoors on a windy day.

A faux-stone pot—here, in Coralstone—lends texture to any color scheme. Add a contrasting color accent with a green plant or coordinate with pink-toned flowers.

PROJECT

making a **weathered** stone pot

1 Clean and dry the surface of the pot. If it is especially discolored or stained, first paint it with a base coat in a color similar to Weathered Stone. Let it dry. Spray the specialty paint evenly over the pot. You can apply a second coat for a heavier texture. Let the paint dry.

2 Apply clear protector, spraying the dry surface evenly. This will protect the finish from moisture and will make it easier to clean; it is essential if you plan to keep the piece outdoors.

crackle finish for a magazine rack

PAINT ON OLD WOOD THAT HAS BEEN left unprotected from the elements or extremes of heat and cold often cracks in an interesting random pattern. This weathered look is popular in some styles of interior decor, especially rustic or country looks where age carries an association of rich history. To replicate this effect on newer items like the magazine rack shown here, simply spray two different colors of special crackling paint, in sequence, over your item. The greater the contrast between the colors, the more dramatic the crackle effect will be.

Crackle glazes can also be brushed on in a multistep process, but this spray method is something anyone can do quickly and easily to give character to everyday items. It is intended for items used indoors or in a protected outdoor location like a covered porch.

1 Sand the surface to remove any splinters and roughness. Wipe with a tack cloth. Spray the base coat evenly over the magazine rack. Let it dry completely, but no more than 48 hours.

TOOLS AND MATERIALS

- Unfinished wood or secondhand magazine rack
- Sandpaper
- Tack cloth
- Decorative Effects Weathered Crackle Base Coat, Ivory Hue (Valspar)
- Decorative Effects Weathered Crackle top coat, Billiard Green (Valspar)
- Decorative Effects acrylic interior clear protector (Valspar)

2 Spray the top coat lightly and evenly over the entire surface. Stop spraying when the surface begins to crack. Let it dry.

3 Apply a coat of clear protector to seal the color.

LOWE'S QUICK TIP

When you're finished, always turn the can upside down and hold down the spray button until all of the product is out of the tip. This will keep the spray tip from clogging.

decorative
effects for walls

A SOLID COLOR WALL CAN BE VERY ATTRACTIVE, BUT WHEN you want to add more character to a room, a faux finish can provide that extra personality. Once reserved for the most ornate villas and estates, decorative painting has gone mainstream, from tract homes to city townhouses.

This chapter includes instructions for creating the most popular special effects for walls, from relatively simple ones to those that take considerably more time, patience, and expertise. (Two other textured finish effects for walls appear with the easy projects, on pages 132–133.) In all projects that use translucent glaze, you have the option of working with a commercially prepared glaze or mixing your own (see page 71). Most techniques call for a base coat below the decorative one. For information on how to prepare walls and paint on a base coat, see pages 80-93.

Some effects can be achieved in more than one way, with subtly different results; where this is so, you'll find directions for each method. You can also vary the effect by applying a technique only to a portion of the wall, such as the frieze (the top 10 to 12 inches) or the dado (the bottom third). The tools and materials you'll need can be purchased at any Lowe's.

Always wear latex gloves for projects with oil-base finishes to protect your hands from harmful chemicals as well as hard-to-remove color. Also, try to finish an entire wall in one session; taking a break before it is done will make the final finish uneven.

start with a brush

colorwashing

New walls take on the look of old-world plaster with a buff glaze color-washed over a lighter buff paint—the perfect treatment to accompany rough timber beams.

ONE OF THE MOST POPULAR TECH-niques for creating a mottled, aged wall texture is colorwashing. Colorwashing is also one of the easiest techniques; you just apply a glaze over a base coat to produce a variety of shades of color across the surface of the wall. The result can provide a dramatic background for very ornate mouldings in a classical setting, or it can imitate the old plaster walls of a European farmhouse or Spanish Colonial. Color-washing also tends to hide flaws, making it ideal for walls that are not in good cosmetic condition. For a more rustic look, apply a textured lime wash before color-washing (see page 144).

Color Matches **Walls: base coat: Valspar Victorian Light Sand; glaze: Decorative Effects Translucent Glaze Buff**

Usually, colors for colorwashing are in a single family, with the glaze a darker shade of the base color. A light glaze over a darker base can also be effective, but not all such combinations work well, and the result can be chalky. You can also use more than one color of glaze (see page 143). You may be able to find paint chips or palette cards showing decorative color combinations. If not, always experiment before committing to a particular palette.

Your brushstrokes can be crude as you apply the glaze, but watch for drips and immediately brush them out. Drips indicate a glaze is too thin. A commercially prepared glaze should not pose this problem, but if you've mixed your own glaze, thicken it with more paint. See pages 70–71 for basic information on glazes.

Above: Lime wash softens color with a white overlayer (see page 144). Here, the base coat is Valspar's Decorative Effects Full Moon.

Color Matches Wall: base coat: Valspar Bronco; glaze: Decorative Effects Translucent Glaze Maroon

Left: A red-orange glaze over a brown base provides warm, rich texture to a sitting room. The walls take color cues from the brown tones of the hardwood floor.

LOWE'S QUICK TIP
When you make your own glaze from scratch, you can control its thickness. See page 71 for glaze recipes.

colorwashing with one color glaze

TOOLS AND MATERIALS

- Latex gloves
- Latex paint, satin
- Paint bucket, grid, brushes, and roller for base coat
- Painter's masking tape
- Translucent color glaze
- Paint tray with liners
- 4-inch colorwashing brushes

IN THIS TYPE OF COLORWASHING, THE wall is "washed" with a translucent glaze in broad crisscross strokes over a dry base coat. The soft look can be increased by brushing the damp surface with a dry brush or gently blotting it with cheesecloth before the glaze begins to dry. To avoid lap marks and inconsistent texture, be sure to complete one wall before going to the next.

A glaze of Mayan Treasure colorwashed over Moonshine—both Olympic Paint colors—adds the right amount of warmth to a dining room. This color combination would be ideal for a Tuscan-style home.

1 Apply the base coat and let it dry completely. Tape off any adjacent surfaces you don't wish to paint. Pour some glaze into a paint tray and load a colorwashing brush. (To mix your own glaze, see page 71.)

Color Matches for both photos **Base coat: Valspar Pollen; glaze: Decorative Effects Translucent Glaze Moss**

2 Starting near, but not in, the top corner of the wall, hold the brush by the base and loosely brush the glaze over a 3-foot-square section with sweeping crisscross strokes. Move your wrist to vary the angle. Leave large spaces between strokes while the brush is fully loaded; fill in spaces and blend your brushstrokes as the brush becomes less saturated. Work the glaze into and away from the corners only after the brush has less paint on it. (If necessary, you can use a dry paintbrush to pull any buildup of paint away from the corner or edges of the wall.)

3 When you begin new 3-foot-square sections, vary the starting points both vertically and horizontally to avoid noticeable demarcations. Always begin at the center of the section, waiting until the brush is less saturated to work back to the last previously completed section and blend your strokes into it. Complete the wall in 3-foot-square sections. Remove the masking tape and allow the finish to dry.

colorwashing with two glazes

IF YOU FEEL CONFIDENT IN YOUR colorwashing ability, you can add a second glaze to give the wall more depth. Work in 3-foot-square sections of wall at a time. Apply the lighter color glaze first in very broad crisscross strokes, leaving plenty of uncovered areas between strokes; you should cover roughly half of the section. When the glaze is exhausted from the brush, dip it into the second color of glaze and apply it in a similar manner to the open areas. Don't overlap the two except to blend the edges. While the glazes are still wet, use a softening brush or piece of dry cheesecloth to dab the glazes and blend the brushstrokes.

Color Match Wall base coat: Valspar Blue Silk

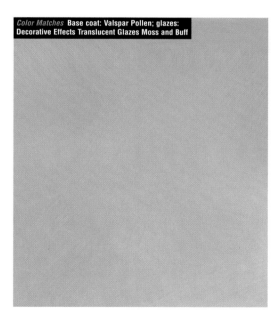

Color Matches Base coat: Valspar Pollen; glazes: Decorative Effects Translucent Glazes Moss and Buff

Left: Here the base coat and green glaze shown on the previous page have been blended with an off-white glaze. The final effect is light and airy, with evident brushstrokes.

Above: Two shades of blue colorwashed on the wall create an informal effect. The moulding has been distressed (see pages 192–193) using a blue base coat topped with a white glaze.

TOOLS AND MATERIALS

- Latex gloves
- Latex paint, satin
- Paint bucket, grid, brushes, and roller for base coat
- Painter's masking tape
- 2 translucent color glazes
- Paint trays with liners
- 4-inch colorwashing brushes
- Softening brush or cheesecloth

LOWE'S QUICK TIP

If you are dealing with a large wall space or two colors of glaze, try to have a second person work with you, either working along other edges or applying the second color.

colorwashing over a **lime-washed** wall

TOOLS AND MATERIALS

- Latex gloves
- Latex paint, satin
- Paint bucket, grid, brushes, and roller for base coat
- Painter's masking tape
- Lime wash
- Paint trays with liners
- Translucent color glaze
- 4-inch colorwashing brushes
- Cheesecloth

LIME WASH ADDS A LAYER OF WHITE texture over the base coat. It softens color and creates the illusion of aged plaster. You can get a similar result by applying a skim coat of joint compound, but lime wash is less labor-intensive. Applying color glaze at the same time as the lime wash can create an old-world effect, as shown here (Valspar's Textured Lime Wash is applied over Decorative Effects Base Coat in Full Moon; the glaze is Burnt Sienna). Lime wash can also be used by itself over a pastel base coat to create a hazy wall finish.

1 Apply the base coat and let it dry completely. Tape off any adjacent surfaces you don't wish to paint. Pour some lime wash into one paint tray and glaze into another. (To mix your own glaze, see page 71.)

2 Use a colorwashing brush to lightly apply lime wash. Lime wash dries quickly, so work in small areas and remove any unwanted buildup immediately with a dry paintbrush. Brush the lime wash in large crisscross strokes, leaving some space between strokes for the glaze.

LOWE'S QUICK TIP

Occasionally stand back and check that you are applying the glaze in a random yet consistent manner.

3 When you have no more lime wash on the brush, dip it in the glaze and apply the glaze in the same X pattern in the spaces you left open. Continue until you have brushed most of the glaze from the brush and then use it to lightly blend the glaze into the lime wash while both are still damp.

4 Repeat the process in small sections across the wall, applying more or less lime wash or glaze to achieve an effect that pleases you. Soften any heavy areas of color or texture with a wad of dry cheesecloth. Remove the masking tape and allow the finish to dry.

stippling

THE TECHNIQUE KNOWN AS STIPPLING results in a subtle, suede-like texture that takes more patience than expertise. You simply bounce a special stippling brush against the surface in a gentle pouncing motion so that just the tips of the brush touch the surface. This creates a pattern of fine dots or flecks of color that leaves just enough of the base color showing through to soften the look.

With stippling, you have several options in choosing a color combination. You can highlight the texture with bold colors of glaze over a white base coat or, conversely, light glazes over a bold base coat. Darker tones over lighter tones of the same color produce a more subtle effect. Experiment with unexpected combinations for a unique look. Stippling will highlight every flaw on

Color Matches Wall above chair rail: base coat: Valspar Apricot Cream; glaze: Decorative Effects Translucent Glaze Maize; wainscot and moulding: Valspar Apricot Cream

a wall, so this is a technique best saved for those that are in good condition.

The following pages show three methods of stippling—stippling "on" or "off" with a brush and stippling off with a small hot-dog foam roller. Each produces its own slightly different result.

Above: Stippling can also be done with cheesecloth. The technique creates a subtle texture appropriate for this traditional dining room.

Left: Using more than one decorative technique on a wall adds visual interest. Here, the whole wall has Valspar's Keepsake as a base coat, topped with Decorative Effects Maroon glaze, but the stippled lower third of the wall is darker than the airy colorwashed upper portion.

stippling on

TOOLS AND MATERIALS

- Latex gloves
- Latex paint, satin
- Paint bucket, grid, brushes, and roller for base coat
- Painter's masking tape
- Translucent color glaze
- Paint tray with liners
- Stippling brush
- Paper towels or newspaper
- Colorwashing brush

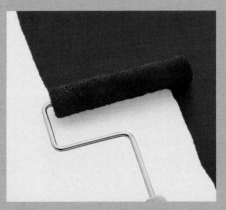

1 Apply the base coat and let it dry completely. Tape off any adjacent surfaces you don't wish to paint. Pour some glaze into a paint tray. (To mix your own glaze, see page 71.) This is Decorative Effects Base Coat in Surrey Green; the glaze is Buff.

2 Dip a stippling brush into the color glaze and blot the excess on a paper towel or newspaper. Begin to stipple the surface, pouncing the brush lightly against the wall so that only the tips of the bristles touch. Create a random pattern by continually changing the angles of your wrist and elbow.

stippling off

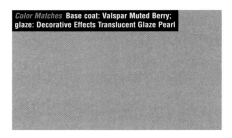

Color Matches Base coat: Valspar Muted Berry; glaze: Decorative Effects Translucent Glaze Pearl

When a lighter glaze is stippled off a darker base, the visual texture is soft and subtle.

TOOLS AND MATERIALS

Latex gloves	Paint tray with
Latex paint,	liners
satin	2-inch foam
Paint bucket,	brush
grid, brushes,	Roller
and roller for	Stippling
base coat	brush
Painter's	Paper towels
masking tape	or newspaper
Translucent	Colorwashing
color glaze	brush

1 Apply the base coat and let it dry completely. Tape off any adjacent surfaces you don't wish to paint. Pour some glaze into a paint tray. (If you are mixing your own glaze, follow the recipe on page 71.) Using a foam brush, cut the glaze into a top corner; cut in 18 inches along the top of the wall. Apply two roller widths of glaze from top to bottom, stopping 2 inches above the baseboard (you'll move glaze into that area as you stipple). Starting in the top corner and working out and down, immediately stipple off the wet glaze by pouncing a dry stippling brush on the surface, allowing only the tips of the bristles to touch. Leave a 6-inch-wide area along the outside edge of the wet glaze untouched.

2 Occasionally remove excess glaze from the brush by gently wiping and pouncing it on a paper towel or newspaper. When you reach a tight spot or a corner, change to a clean colorwashing brush and pounce it into the area.

LOWE'S QUICK TIP

For larger areas, work with a partner. One of you can roll on the glaze and the other can stipple it. This lets you work more quickly before the glaze dries.

3 Continue to apply glaze, shifting the position of your arm as you move across the wall. Use a colorwashing brush to stipple in corners or other tight areas. Remove the masking tape and allow the finish to dry.

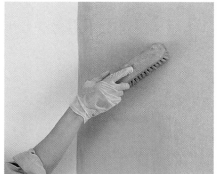

3 After you finish one section, roll another two widths of glaze from the top to the bottom of the wall, butting your roller up to the edge of the 6-inch undisturbed wet glaze. Be sure not to overlap the glaze, however. Working from top to bottom, begin stippling off along the edge of the previously worked section and continue stippling from top to bottom in one pass, leaving a new 6-inch band of undisturbed glaze at the outside edge. Work across the wall in the same way, stopping only when you have completed the wall. Remove the tape and allow the finish to dry.

stippling with a roller

TOOLS AND MATERIALS

- Latex gloves
- Latex paint, satin
- Paint bucket, grid, brushes, and roller for base coat
- Painter's masking tape
- Translucent color glaze
- Paint tray with liners
- 2-inch foam brush
- Hot-dog rollers
- Paper towels

1 Apply the base coat and let it dry completely. Tape off any adjacent surfaces you don't wish to paint. Pour some glaze into a paint tray. (To mix your own glaze, see page 71.)

3 Using a clean, dry hot-dog roller, lightly roll over the glaze. Keep rolling over the same area until you remove enough glaze to produce the desired stippling effect. When the roller becomes loaded with glaze, blot it by rolling it over a paper towel.

2 Using a foam brush lightly loaded with glaze, cut in the glaze along the top of the wall and the baseboard for about 18 inches from the corner. Load a hot-dog roller with glaze and roll it from ceiling to baseboard along the corner, re-rolling the area until you fill the 18-inch cut-in section completely.

4 Starting adjacent to the area you just rolled, cut in and roll glaze onto another section without directly overlapping. Blend the glaze into the previously rolled section and roll off the glaze with a clean roller as in Step 3. Repeat until the wall is completed. Remove the masking tape and allow the finish to dry.

A roller produces a much finer haze of color than the stippling brush. This technique used over a vibrant paint can subdue and even rescue an effect that is too busy or bright.

Color Matches **Base coat: Valspar Muted Berry; glaze: Decorative Effects Translucent Glaze Pearl**

spattering

Below: The impact of spattering varies depending on the colors used. Here the same spatter colors were used over an off-white base, top, and a green base, bottom.

Below right: The spattering on this cottage guest room is heavier on the lower part of the wall, fading to a pale mist above.

SPATTERING IS REMINISCENT OF THOSE early days of elementary school, when you sprayed paint on the kid next to you while the teacher wasn't looking. The technique—pulling on the bristles to let fly a splattering of paint—is almost the same. But when you are spattering an entire wall, you pull a stick across the bristles rather than using your fingers.

Although it is a simple process that can produce a playful effect, spattering can be a remarkably sophisticated finish. You can apply it over a solid color or over another decorative finish. You can spatter a single color, or a whole palette of different ones.

This is a technique that is messy and by its nature imprecise. It can be carried out by several people working side by side. Just make sure everyone's wearing protective clothing to avoid getting more paint on the painters than on the wall.

TOOLS AND MATERIALS

☐ Latex gloves	☐ Canvas drop cloth
☐ Latex paint, satin	☐ Translucent color
☐ Paint bucket, grid,	glaze
brushes, and roller	☐ Plastic container
for base coat	☐ 3-inch chip brush
☐ Pre-taped plastic	☐ Stirring stick or
drop cloths (see	long-handled
page 74)	paintbrush

Color Matches Base coat: American Tradition Bone White; glaze: Decorative Effects Translucent Glazes Maize, Maroon, and Mocha

Color Matches Base coat: Laura Ashley Home Dark Green 5; glazes: Decorative Effects Translucent Glazes Maize, Maroon, and Mocha

Color Matches Base coat: American Tradition White; glazes: Decorative Effects Translucent Glazes Stone Gray and Slate Blue

1 Apply the base coat and let it dry completely. Using pre-taped plastic drop cloths, mask the ceiling, baseboard, and walls adjacent to where you'll be working. Cover the floor with a canvas drop cloth. Pour some glaze into a plastic container. (If you wish to make your own glaze from scratch so you can control its thickness, start with a mixture of 2 parts latex paint to 1 part water for this project.)

Color Matches for all photos **Base coat: Laura Ashley Home Dark Green 5; glazes: Decorative Effects Translucent Glazes Maize, Maroon, and Mocha**

LOWE'S QUICK TIP

To get larger flecks, tap the handle of the loaded brush against the spatter stick, instead of pulling the stick through the bristles.

2 Test your spattering by placing some scrap paper on the floor. Dip a chip brush into the glaze. Hold the brush about 18 inches above the paper with a narrow side facing you. Use a stirring stick or a long-handled paintbrush as your spatter stick, placing it on the far side of the loaded brush and perpendicular to it. Pull the spatter stick toward you across the bristle tips, releasing a spray of paint flecks onto the paper. For larger dots, stand farther away; for smaller ones, stand closer. Once you produce the size of dots that you want, always keep that same distance.

3 Reload the brush and remove the excess paint by spattering a scrap of paper. Hold the loaded brush upright so that the narrow edge is parallel to the wall and fairly close to the ceiling. Stand the same distance away from the wall as you did from the paper in Step 2. As before, pull the spatter stick toward you across the bristles, releasing a spray of paint flecks on the wall. Reposition the brush to the side or below that part of the wall and repeat. Reload the brush when flecks become too small. Continue until the remainder of the wall is spattered, and let it dry.

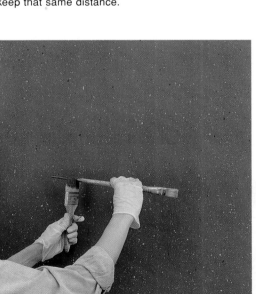

4 If you are using more than one color of glaze, let the glaze dry between colors and repeat the process with each of the glazes. Stand back and observe the effect. If you wish, spatter on more of any or all of the glazes. Remove the masking tape and allow the finish to dry.

LOWE'S QUICK TIP

You can also spatter a floor or other horizontal surface. Since there's no danger of dripping, the glaze can be thinner than for a wall. Be aware that a thinner glaze will spatter in larger flecks.

dragging

DRAGGING GIVES THE IMPRESSION OF an elegantly woven fabric like linen or silk, at a fraction of the cost. The technique has its origins in the eighteenth century; it still imparts classical elegance when paired with traditional mouldings. To create the desired effect, you drag a brush straight down through wet glaze to create fine striations. This requires a steady hand, speed, practice, and, ideally, at least one helper—you'll get the best results when one person rolls on the glaze and the other drags the brush through it.

In dragging, it is most common to use either base coat and glaze colors with similar tonal qualities or a dark color over a light base. However, highly contrasting base and glaze colors can be very striking.

TOOLS AND MATERIALS

- Latex gloves
- Latex paint, satin
- Paint bucket, grid, brushes, and roller for base coat
- Painter's masking tape
- Plumb bobs
- Translucent color glaze
- Paint tray with liners
- 2-inch foam brush
- Roller
- 3-inch paintbrushes
- Rags

The denim effect on these bedroom walls was created by dragging Olympic's Teeny Bikini over a base coat of Creamy White.

LOWE'S QUICK TIP
To create the look of linen, apply a second layer of glaze after the first one has dried and drag it horizontally, perpendicular to the first vertical striations.

1 Apply the base coat; let it dry completely. Tape off any adjacent surfaces you don't wish to paint. Tape plumb bobs to the ceiling at 2-foot intervals, a few inches in front of the wall you'll be painting. Pour some glaze into a paint tray. (To mix your own glaze, see page 71.)

2 Using a foam brush, cut the glaze into the corner where you'll begin; also cut in for 18 inches along the top and bottom of the wall. Load a roller with glaze and roll two roller widths of glaze from top to bottom, reloading as needed.

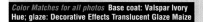

Color Matches for all photos **Base coat: Valspar Ivory Hue; glaze: Decorative Effects Translucent Glaze Maize**

The brushstrokes leave very fine and subtle stripes of color that make the finished wall interesting but not busy.

3 Starting at the top corner, place the tip of a paintbrush on the wall just below the ceiling and against the corner. (The tape on the adjacent wall will allow you to drag right into the corner). Pressing the body of the brush toward the wall and extending your arm out straight, drag the brush down to the baseboard in one continuous stroke. Use the plumb bobs as guides to keep your lines as straight as possible. Wipe the brush on a rag as you work; when the rag no longer cleans the glaze off the brush, switch to a second brush. Drag a second band adjacent and parallel to the first. Continue to drag the rest of the applied glaze, leaving a 2-inch-wide wet edge. Re-drag the same area, removing as much glaze as needed to create a fine striated pattern.

4 Cut in another 18-inch section along the top and bottom of the wall adjacent to the first section. Roll two roller widths of glaze from top to bottom. Drag the wet glaze, starting with the wet edge of the previous section, as in Step 3. Repeat the process until the wall is complete. Remove the masking tape and allow the finish to dry.

LOWE'S QUICK TIP

For a lighter effect, drag your brush over the same area three or four times.

try a tool

rubbing

RUBBING A GLAZE ON OR OFF WITH A cotton knit rag produces an effect similar to colorwashing, but a bit lighter and more translucent. You'll also see no brush marks, just swirled clouds of color.

There are two methods of rubbing, which yield different results. In "rubbing on," you rub the glaze on top of the base coat. In "rubbing off," you first brush the glaze over the base coat and then remove it with a rag. Rubbing off produces a more blended look than rubbing on, and because you start with more paint on the wall, less of the base coat shows through.

Choose base coat and glaze color combinations as you would for a conventional colorwashing project (see page 141).

You can re-create the freshness of a clear sky when a blue glaze is rubbed over a lighter blue wall.

Color Matches **Base coat: Valspar Whimsical; glaze: Decorative Effects Translucent Glaze Slate Blue**

rubbing **on**

With rubbing, areas
of deeper color
blend naturally into
areas of faded color.

Color Matches Base coat: Valspar Whimsical; glaze:
Decorative Effects Translucent Glaze Slate Blue

TOOLS AND MATERIALS

- Latex gloves
- Latex paint, satin
- Paint bucket, grid, brushes, and roller for base coat
- Painter's masking tape
- Cotton knit rags
- Translucent color glaze
- Paint tray with liners
- 2-inch foam brush
- House painter's brush

1 Apply the base coat and let it dry completely. Tape off any adjacent surfaces you don't wish to paint.

Color Match **Wall: Earth Elements Stonecrop**

2 Flatten several cotton knit rags and fold each to about 6 inches square. Stack them at the center of an unfolded rag. Wrap this rag around the stack of folded ones. Wad up the excess and grasp it in your working hand. As you work, you can rearrange the wrapping to expose new sections until the entire rag is too soiled to be of further use. Then use a new one.

3 Pour some glaze into a paint tray. (To mix your own glaze, see page 71.) Using a foam brush, cut the glaze into the corner where you'll begin (extend the glaze slightly onto the adjacent wall if you will be rubbing it as well); reload the brush as needed. Using your wadded-up rag, rub the glaze with small circular movements, working from the corner toward the center of the wall. Remove any excess glaze remaining in the corner by pouncing up and down with a house painter's brush.

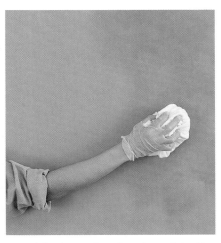

4 Dip the rag into the glaze; dab off the excess on the clean side of the paint tray. Starting in the corner you've just cut in, place the rag on the wall about a foot from the rubbed corner and rub the glaze toward the corner, using small circular movements to blend the new glaze into the edges of the previously rubbed section. Continue spreading out the glaze in all directions, until all the glaze on your rag has been applied. Working in irregular 3-foot sections, repeat this process, alternately working next to and beneath each previously rubbed section. Always cut in the glaze with a foam brush at corners. Remove the masking tape and allow the finish to dry.

rubbing Off

TOOLS AND MATERIALS

- Latex gloves
- Latex paint, satin
- Paint bucket, grid, brushes, and roller for base coat
- Painter's masking tape
- Cotton knit rags
- Translucent color glaze
- Paint tray with liners
- 2-inch foam brush
- House painter's brush

1 Follow Steps 1 and 2 for Rubbing On (see page 153), then pour some glaze into a paint tray. (To mix your own glaze, see page 71.)

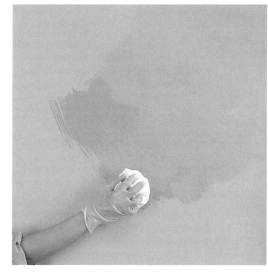

2 Starting at the top of the wall by a corner, cut in the glaze with a foam brush; extend it slightly onto the adjacent wall if you will be rubbing it as well. Using prepared rags, rub off the glaze with small circular movements to fade out the edges. Use a house painter's brush to pounce out any glaze that accumulates in the corner.

4 Repeat the process, alternating sections next to and beneath each previously rubbed section. Remove the masking tape and allow the finish to dry.

Color Matches for all photos **Base coat: Valspar Yellowstone; glaze: Decorative Effects Translucent Glaze Mocha**

3 Starting 6 to 12 inches from the rubbed-off corner, brush on some glaze, using crisscross strokes over an irregular 2-foot-square section. With the rag, rub off the glaze, blending it into the corner as well as the untouched adjacent areas.

LOWE'S QUICK TIP

When you're blending into more than one adjacent area, don't try to refine one edge at a time. Instead, develop a rhythm for lifting the rag and working back and forth between the previously worked edges.

Rubbing off will create a more blended look that is closer to the glaze color than the base color.

sponging

SPONGING IS A VERSATILE DECORATIVE painting technique that produces a great variety of effects, depending on the colors you choose and your method of application. "Sponging on" several colors of glaze can result in a finish with greater depth, while "sponging off" a single glaze color yields a subtle, dappled look.

Natural sponges were once living creatures with their own shapes, so each one imparts its own unique characteristics to the wall. Working with two or three different sponges will avoid a repetitive pattern.

Color choice is one key to success. With the sponge-on technique, imperfections are eye-catching, so it takes a bit of skill to apply contrasting hues attractively. The last color you apply will be the most dominant. An easier approach is to choose your base coat and glaze from the same color family. With sponging off, on the other hand, the color values of the base coat and glaze must be very different or the effect will not be noticeable.

PROJECT

sponging **on**

An off-white glaze (Valspar's American Tradition Blazing Star mixed with translucent pearl glaze) over a deep yellow base (American Tradition Summer Haze) tones down the overall color effect. This technique is a great way to lighten any painted wall that appears too dark. For more depth and a livelier effect, sponge on two or three different colors that have the same intensity.

Color Matches for all photos **Base coat: Valspar Summer Haze; glaze: Decorative Effects Translucent Pearl tinted to Valspar Blazing Star**

TOOLS AND MATERIALS

- Latex gloves
- Latex paint, satin
- Paint bucket, grid, brushes, and roller for base coat
- Painter's masking tape
- Translucent color glaze
- Paint tray with liners
- Large natural sea sponges with medium pores

1 Apply the base coat and let it dry completely. Tape off any adjacent surfaces you don't wish to paint. Pour some glaze into a paint tray. (To mix your own glaze, see page 71.) Dip a sponge into the mixture and squeeze out any excess glaze. The sponge should be loaded but not clogged. Blot it on the tray and test it on paper until you can get a neat pattern without smears or blobs.

PROJECT CONTINUES ➡

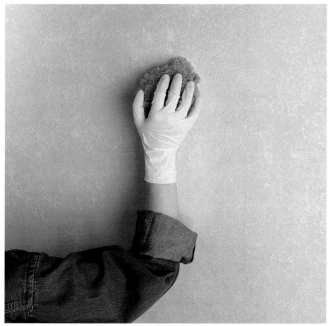

2 Starting with a 3-foot-square area, lightly pounce the surface with the sponge, using quick movements of your wrist and rotating the sponge each time you lift it. Space the dabs approximately 3 inches apart in a random pattern. Reload the sponge whenever the impressions begin to lighten. Fill in spaces until the surface is evenly covered; you should not be able to see where one impression stops and another begins. Leave the leading edge of each section irregular so you can blend the next one with it smoothly. Continue repeating this technique section by section until the wall is covered. You can handle corners and edges as you go, using the methods in Step 4, or wait until the end.

3 Once all sections are completed, stand back and look for gaps and uneven areas. Fill in the gaps and blend in the uneven areas with a sponge that is just barely dampened with glaze. Pounce lightly and avoid overlapping covered areas, which would increase their color intensity.

4 For corners and edges along the ceiling and trim, tear a 3-inch piece off a large sponge. Load it with paint and dab it into the corners and along edges. Remove the masking tape and allow the finish to dry.

sponging Off

1 Apply the base coat and let it dry completely. Tape off any adjacent surfaces you don't wish to paint. Pour some glaze into a paint tray. (To mix your own glaze, see page 71.)

2 Using a foam brush, cut the glaze into the top corner where you'll begin; also cut in 18 inches along the top and bottom of the wall. Load a roller with glaze and roll two roller widths of glaze from top to bottom, moving the roller in a wavy path to create an uneven edge. Reload the roller as needed.

TOOLS AND MATERIALS

- Latex gloves
- Latex paint, satin
- Paint bucket, grid, brushes, and roller for base coat
- Painter's masking tape
- Translucent color glaze
- Paint tray with liners
- Foam brush
- Roller
- Large natural sea sponges with medium pores
- Bucket filled with water
- Cotton rag

Color Matches for all photos **Base coat: Valspar Whippoorwill; glaze: Decorative Effects Translucent Glaze Maize**

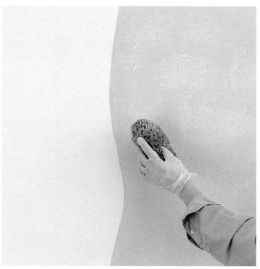

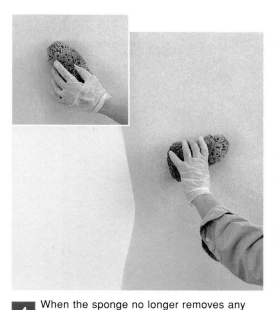

3 Dip a sponge into the water bucket and squeeze it until it no longer drips. Pounce the sponge on the wet glaze and then blot the sponge on a rag. Continue pouncing and blotting, working in 2-foot-square sections and removing the glaze in a loose spiral pattern. Work in and out of the corner as an extension of your spirals, scrunching up the sponge so you can dab it into the corner to remove the glaze. The more you pounce, the lighter the effect will be.

4 When the sponge no longer removes any glaze, rinse it in water and wring it out. Resume pouncing in a less obvious area since a clean sponge will remove more glaze. Then pounce over the rest of the glazed area to fill in the spiral, rotating the sponge lightly on the wall. After this section is completed, roll on another ceiling-to-floor swath and repeat the sponging. Continue until the entire wall is complete. Remove the masking tape and allow the finish to dry.

Sponging off leaves a subtler visual texture than sponging on, more like stippling and ragging.

LOWE'S QUICK TIP

If you rinse the sponge after every few pounces, more of the base coat will show through. However, to do this successfully, you'll have to work very quickly.

The shading variations created by ragging give a natural texture to these terra-cotta walls. Note the faux-stone pattern on the fireplace surround, highlighted by a monogram that appears to be carved.

Color Matches Walls: base coat: Valspar Burnt Cumin; glaze: Decorative Effects Translucent Glaze Burnt Sienna

LOWE'S QUICK TIP

Try ragging with other materials such as leather scraps, chamois, burlap, or bubble wrap; each material will leave its own unique imprint.

ragging

SUBTLER THAN SPONGING, RAGGING uses a paper towel, rag, or plastic sheet to create a refined finish like crushed velvet or soft suede. You can "rag on," using the same technique described on pages 155–156 for sponging on; "rag off," the traditional method described here; or "rag roll" with a rolled-up cloth (see page 161).

The results will vary depending on the colors you use, the amount of glaze you remove, and the shape and texture of the material you use to do the ragging. Ragging with plastic leaves a bolder texture than ragging with paper or cloth. Rag rolling is much crisper, with a more identifiable pattern.

traditional **ragging**

TOOLS AND MATERIALS

- Latex gloves
- Latex paint, satin
- Paint bucket, grid, brushes, and rollers for base coat
- Painter's masking tape
- Translucent color glaze
- Paint trays with liners
- Paper towels
- 2-inch foam brush
- Roller

1 Apply the base coat and let it dry completely. Tape off any adjacent surfaces you don't wish to paint. Pour some glaze into a paint tray. (To mix your own glaze, see page 71.)

3 Beginning in the corner and working from top to bottom, pounce your paper-towel "rag" on the wet glaze, using quick movements of your wrist. Bunch the rag as necessary so that it fits into the ceiling and vertical corners. Working in an area approximately 2 feet deep, space the dabs 3 to 6 inches apart; don't work onto the outside edge of the glaze. Continue to dab between dabs until you've touched all the open spaces. Vary the pattern by rotating and rearranging the rag after lifting it. When the rag becomes saturated with glaze, change to a fresh one. After you complete one section, repeat the process, ragging beneath the previously worked area until you reach the baseboard.

2 Tear off about ten 5-towel lengths of paper towels. Wad up one length as your first "rag" and keep the others nearby. Using a foam brush, cut the glaze into the corner where you'll begin; also cut in for 18 inches along the top and bottom of the wall. Load a roller with glaze and roll two roller widths of glaze from top to bottom.

4 Using a foam brush, cut in another 18-inch section along the ceiling and baseboard next to the first section. Roll two roller widths of glaze from top to bottom. Pounce a rag from ceiling to floor along the edge of the previous section to blend it with the fresh glaze. Then rag the width of the glaze from ceiling to floor, working in 2-foot-square sections. Continue ragging until the wall is complete. Remove the masking tape and allow the finish to dry.

LOWE'S QUICK TIP

The bunching of the paper-towel rag gives this technique its character. Instead of creating a tight ball, grab the rag loosely so that it retains its varied folds. For a slightly different look, use 2-foot-square cloth rags instead of paper towels.

Color Matches for all photos **Base coat: Earth Elements Oasis; glaze: Decorative Effects Translucent Glaze Buff**

A ragged surface should have even texture, with no open areas of base color showing through.

ragging with a plastic sheet

A plastic-ragged wall can offer all the texture you need in a room. While it looks messy to do, it's no messier than using a cloth rag (see opposite page), and is a bit quicker to complete.

Color Matches Base coat: Earth Elements Oasis; glaze: Decorative Effects Translucent Glaze Buff

Ragging with shades of beige and brown results in a paper-like surface and earthy color, an appealing complement to the wrought-iron hardware.

TOOLS AND MATERIALS

- Latex gloves
- Latex paint, satin
- Paint bucket, grid, brushes, and roller for base coat
- Painter's masking tape
- Translucent color glaze
- Paint tray with liners
- 1.5-mil plastic sheeting
- 2-inch foam brush
- Roller

Color Matches Base coat: American Tradition Avalon; glaze: Decorative Effects translucent glaze Mocha

1 Follow Steps 1 and 2 for Traditional Ragging (see page 159), but instead of preparing paper towels, cut several pieces of 1.5-mil plastic sheeting 18 to 24 inches square.

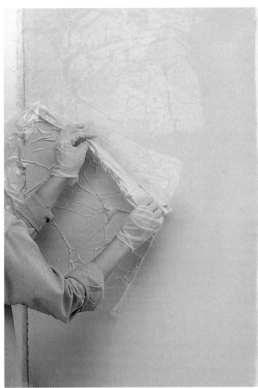

2 Beginning at the ceiling, place a piece of plastic over the glaze as close to the corners and edges as you can. Press down lightly in random areas and peel it off. Reposition the plastic below the area just pressed and repeat. When the plastic becomes saturated, discard it and use a new square. You can reposition the plastic over the same area and press again to even out the effect. If necessary, bunch the plastic to fit into the ceiling and vertical corners.

3 Cut in another 18-inch section along the top and bottom of the wall adjacent to the first section. Roll two roller widths of glaze from top to bottom, reloading as needed. Rag the glaze with plastic sheets as before. Continue in this manner until the wall is complete. Remove the masking tape and allow the finish to dry.

rag rolling

TOOLS AND MATERIALS

- Latex gloves
- Latex paint, satin
- Paint bucket, grid, brushes, and roller for base coat
- Painter's masking tape
- Translucent color glaze
- Paint tray with liners
- Cotton rags
- 2-inch foam brush
- Roller

1 Follow Steps 1 and 2 for Traditional Ragging (see page 159). Fold a 2-foot-square cotton rag in half and twist it lengthwise to form a long loose cylinder. The base coat here is Olympic's 215-3 and the glaze is 218-5.

2 Place the rag at the top of the wall, aligning one end with the corner. Using your fingertips, roll the rag down the wall, working your way to the baseboard. The roll should not extend to the edge of the rolled-on glaze. When the rag stops removing glaze, retwist it to reveal a clean area. When it becomes saturated, switch to a clean rag. Use the end of the cylinder to roll or blot any missed areas in the corners or along edges.

3 Cut in another 18-inch section along the ceiling and baseboard with a foam brush, adjacent to the completed section. Roll two roller widths of glaze from top to bottom, reloading as needed. Roll your rag from ceiling to floor through the glaze, overlapping the previously rolled section. Repeat this process until all the walls are completed. Remove the masking tape and allow the finish to dry.

LOWE'S QUICK TIP

Try rolling diagonally instead of vertically to create a fantasy marble effect. Or change hand angles and positions frequently to add more variety to the pattern.

combing

IN ITS SIMPLEST FORM, COMBING imparts a country style to walls with its traditional linear pattern. But pull your combing tool both horizontally and vertically, or in arcs across the wall, and the finish becomes a very contemporary treatment.

There are a number of different combing tools available in various widths and with different size teeth, each of which produces its own patterns. You can also make combs from plastic lids, cardboard, or even a notched squeegee. Bear in mind, however, that cardboard wears out easily and is not recommended for large areas.

Combing is not for the beginner. It requires uninterrupted lines, so you must complete each floor-to-ceiling section before the glaze dries. As with many of the decorative techniques, choosing a base coat and a glaze in two tones of the same color will produce the most subtle, refined effect.

TOOLS AND MATERIALS

▨ Latex gloves	▨ Paint tray with
▨ Latex paint, satin	liners
▨ Paint bucket, grid,	▨ 2-inch foam brush
brushes, and roller	▨ Roller
for base coat	▨ 3-inch
▨ Painter's masking	paintbrushes
tape	▨ Rags
▨ Plumb bobs	▨ Combing tool
▨ Translucent color	
glaze	

While there should be no demarcation lines on a combed wall, the lines don't have to be perfectly straight. It is important, when you complete Step 3, for the dragged glaze color to be even before you begin combing.

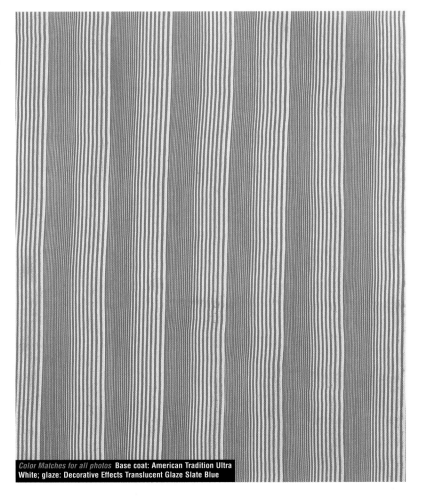

Color Matches for all photos **Base coat: American Tradition Ultra White; glaze: Decorative Effects Translucent Glaze Slate Blue**

1 Apply the base coat and let it dry completely. Tape off any adjacent surfaces you don't wish to paint. Tape the plumb bobs to the ceiling at 2-foot intervals a few inches in front of the wall you'll be painting. Pour some glaze into a paint tray. (To mix your own glaze, see page 71.)

2 Using a foam brush, cut the glaze into the corner where you'll begin. Also cut in for 18 inches along the top and bottom of the wall. Load a roller with glaze and roll two roller widths of glaze from top to bottom, reloading as needed. Be sure to roll the glaze evenly.

LOWE'S QUICK TIP

If you are using a graduated comb, you can alternate the wide and narrow stripes by turning over the comb every time you reposition it at the ceiling. Test the pattern on a piece of cardboard before you begin.

3 Starting at the top corner, place the tip of a paintbrush on the wall just below the ceiling. Pressing the body of the brush toward the wall, drag the brush down to the baseboard in one continuous stroke. Use the plumb bobs as guides to keep your lines as straight as possible. Wipe the brush on a rag. When the rag no longer cleans the glaze off the brush, switch to a second brush. Drag a second band adjacent and parallel to the first. Repeat as needed to drag the rest of the applied glaze, leaving a 2-inch-wide wet edge. Redrag the same area until the glaze is no longer runny.

4 Starting at the top corner of the area you just dragged, hold your combing tool parallel to the ceiling, press the teeth against the wall, and pull the comb straight down to the baseboard. (The tool shown here is a triangular rubber graining comb with graduated teeth.) Clean the comb with a rag. Starting directly next to the area you just completed, comb the adjacent section; do not overlap the pattern. Continue until you have combed all the dragged glaze. Then cut in and roll another section two roller widths wide. Repeat the dragging and combing process, incorporating the wet edge of the previous section. Continue until you have finished the entire wall. Remove the masking tape and allow the finish to dry.

VARIATION

To create an informal plaid effect, use a graduated graining tool (see page 76) to comb the surface vertically and then use it again horizontally while the glaze is still wet.

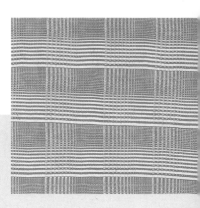

imitations that add atmosphere

creating a **brushed-metal** finish

A RICH METALLIC FINISH LENDS ITSELF to the sleek, clean lines of contemporary decor, providing a handsome contrast to leather, steel, or iron furniture. You can produce the brushed-metal effect that is shown here by using a large wallpaper-smoothing brush to create arcs through a specialty glaze. This project uses one of Valspar's metal glazes, which come in gold, bronze, copper, and silver. If you wish, you can antique the finish with Valspar's Asphaltum antiquing glaze.

TOOLS AND MATERIALS

- Latex gloves
- Decorative Effects base coat (Valspar)
- Paint bucket, grid, brushes, and roller for base coat
- Painter's masking tape
- Metal glaze (Valspar)
- Paint tray with liners
- Foam brush
- 4-inch paintbrush
- Large wallpaper-smoothing brush

The cool and shiny finish of brushed-metal walls can be balanced with neutral tones and soft texture. The base coat here is Valspar's Olive Hint, with Bronze Metal and Patina Glaze.

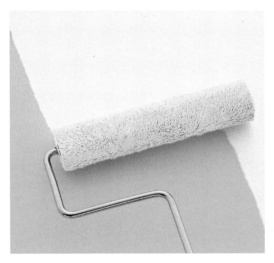

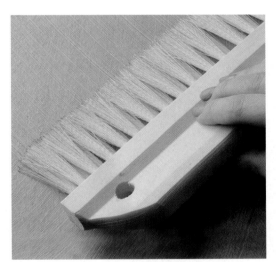

1 Apply the base coat and let it dry completely. Tape off any adjacent surfaces. Pour the metal glaze into a paint tray.

2 Using a foam brush, cut the glaze into the corner where you'll begin; also cut in for 48 inches along the top and bottom of the wall. Load a paintbrush with glaze and cover a 4-foot section of glaze from top to bottom, reloading as needed. Be sure to apply the glaze evenly.

4 Cut in and paint another section of glaze about 4 feet wide, adjacent to the one just completed. Brush overlapping arcs across the wet glaze, including the wet edge of the previous section. Continue until the entire wall is covered. After the first coat has dried, you may add a second coat for a richer metallic look. Remove the masking tape and allow the finish to dry.

3 Starting in a corner or against the ceiling or baseboard, hold the wallpaper-smoothing brush at an angle to the wall and pull it through the wet glaze in a large arc. This sweeping motion allows the base color to show through the glaze in certain areas, creating the look of brushed metal. Lift the brush off the wall, rotate it slightly, and brush another arc that overlaps the bottom edge of the one you just created. Continue until you have covered the wet glaze, leaving about a 6-inch edge of wet glaze untouched. Be sure to rotate the angle of the brush slightly following each arc.

mimicking **venetian plaster**

VENETIAN PLASTER, A MODERN FORM-ulation of an age-old finish, allows you to add rich texture to your walls without requiring special skills or weeks of your time. This project uses a Valspar product that comes in a number of colors to create tone-on-tone variations reminiscent of old-world plaster. The more layers that you apply, the more depth you achieve. Any subtle texture left by the spatula will create the mottling and definition typical of a true plaster finish. The more you work it, the more texture and markings will appear. Burnishing the plaster polishes inert pig-ments, creates areas of high and low gloss, and enhances the textured effect.

Start with a smooth, well-prepared wall surface in which any holes or surface imperfections have been patched and sanded. Apply Venetian plaster only over a matte or flat surface, never over satin, semigloss, or glossy painted surfaces.

TOOLS AND MATERIALS

- Latex gloves
- PVA latex primer or stain-blocking primer
- Paint bucket, grid, brushes, and roller for primer
- Roller with ⅜-inch nap
- Venetian Plaster texture paint (Valspar)
- Steel spatula (see photos at right)
- Bucket filled with water
- Venetian Plaster protective finish (Valspar)

The mottled texture of Venetian plaster creates real shadows across a wall surface. When selecting color (this is Valspar's Decorative Effects Venetian Plaster in Azzurro), make sure you like the way it looks in both dark and light conditions.

1 Apply primer, taking care to produce a smooth, matte, uniform finish. Make sure the primed wall is clean and dry before you begin applying the Venetian Plaster.

2 In an area no larger than 3 feet square, use a roller to apply Venetian plaster to the wall. Working quickly, hold a steel spatula at a 10- to 20-degree angle to the wall and make large overlapping crisscross or arc patterns. This will knock down and smooth the plaster and remove any stipples left by the roller. Skim back over the area with the spatula, making the surface as smooth as possible before it begins to set. Keeping a ragged edge of rolled-on plaster, proceed along the wall section by section to finish applying the first coat. Let the plaster dry approximately 1 to 4 hours, until it has an even matte color.

Clean the spatula in a bucket of water frequently. Any dried product that accumulates on the spatula can scratch and mar the plastered surface. As you work, cover the paint tray with a damp cloth or lid to prevent the plaster from drying.

3 For the second coat, use the spatula to scoop up small amounts of plaster. Apply it over the first coat, working at a 90-degree angle to the wall. Skim the surface to fill in any depressions, leveling and smoothing as you go. (Applying slightly more pressure to the spatula will make a smoother finish.) Let the plaster dry as before. If you wish, apply a third or even a fourth coat. Do not let the final coat dry for more than an hour before proceeding to Step 4.

4 Hold the steel spatula almost flat against the wall and rub it rapidly in a circular motion while applying pressure. This will polish the plaster and enhance the pattern in the finish. If you scratch or nick the surface as you work, patch it immediately with a thin layer of plaster, let the patch dry, and burnish again.

5 Protect areas that will be exposed to moisture or high traffic with the Venetian plaster protective finish, which will result in a slightly deepened color and added sheen. Apply it with the steel spatula as in Step 3; do not roll it on. Let it dry for at least an hour.

LOWE'S QUICK TIP

If you have more texture or spatula lines than you want, lightly sand those areas between coats for a more subtle pattern in the final finish.

emulating natural rock

ONE OF THE MOST POPULAR WALL treatments today is a textured finish that simulates natural rock and can be applied like any paint. The projects shown here use two slightly different products. One is rolled on, while the other has a rolled-on first coat and a brushed-on second coat. Valspar's Decorative Effects Millstone paint comes in muted earth colors with glints of black and white to highlight the color. Valspar's Granite paint, sold under the Signature Colors label, creates the effect of rough-hewn stone. You can ask Lowe's Paint Sales Specialists to mix the paint with Granite Crystals, a companion product, to imitate the shimmer of quartz—or mix in the crystals yourself. Both Millstone and Granite paints work well with contemporary, Mediterranean, and Latin architecture.

TOOLS AND MATERIALS

- Painter's masking tape
- Decorative Effects Millstone paint (Valspar)
- Paint tray
- 2- to 3-inch trim brush
- Roller with ½-inch nap

PROJECT

applying millstone paint

1 Tape off any adjacent surfaces you don't wish to paint. Pour the Millstone paint into a paint tray. With a trim brush, cut in the edges of the wall you are painting. Load a roller and, starting in one corner, roll on the paint in a large W shape. Fill in around the W, completing a 3- by 4-foot section. Continue to work in 3- by 4-foot sections. (See pages 91–92 for more on painting a wall with a roller.)

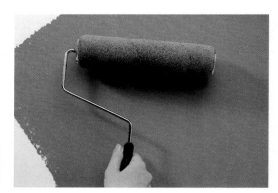

2 While the paint is still wet, roll the entire wall from ceiling to floor in one direction to even out any lap marks. Remove the tape and let the paint dry.

3 Reapply the masking tape. Apply a second coat as in Steps 1 and 2 to provide even coverage and texture. Remove the tape and let the paint dry.

Finely textured Green Moss Millstone paint gives this wall a rugged outdoor look.

Granite paint in Quarry Sand is a perfect complement to the Western decor in this living room.

TOOLS AND
MATERIALS

- Painter's masking tape
- Signature Colors Granite paint (Valspar) with Granite Crystals
- Paint tray
- 2- to 3-inch trim brush
- Roller with 1¼-inch nap
- 3- to 4-inch paintbrush

PROJECT

applying **granite** paint

1 Tape off any adjacent surfaces you don't wish to paint. If you wish to use Granite Crystals, and didn't have them mixed into the paint at the store, stir them in.

2 Pour the paint into a paint tray. With a trim brush, cut in the edges of the wall you are painting. Load a roller and, starting in one corner, roll on the paint in a large W shape. Fill in around the W. Continue, working in 3- by 4-foot sections. (See pages 91–92 for more on painting a wall with a roller.) Remove the tape and let the paint dry.

3 Reapply the tape. Starting near, but not in, the top corner of the wall, hold a 3- to 4-inch paintbrush by the base and loosely brush paint over a 3-foot-square section with sweeping crisscross strokes. The technique is the same as for colorwashing with a single glaze (see page 142). When the wall is finished, remove the tape and let the paint dry.

producing a **marble** finish

MARBLE IS A HEAVILY VEINED STONE with distinctive patterns that can add classical sophistication to a formal room. It is too expensive for most homeowners to use liberally, but luckily it is not that difficult to imitate on wood or other smooth surfaces. Marble finish is a detail that is most effective in small doses, however. Use it sparingly where natural stone might logically be found. Wall panels, fireplace surrounds, columns, or mouldings are all good candidates for faux marble.

Since marble comes in hundreds of different colors, you have great freedom of choice in planning your finish. For the best results, spend some time looking over the veining and color variations of real marble, either in photographs or in samples such as tiles at a store. The following pages show how to create a yellow sienna faux-marble finish. Once it is thoroughly dry, be sure to cover it with a transparent coating, as described, to give it a uniform "polished stone" sheen and to protect the finished design.

Right: A surface painted with a sienna marble finish (see pages 172–173) is informal enough for a bright family room, but can also provide an attractive counterpoint in a more formal setting.

Far right: Faux marbling on wood trim adds texture and pattern to a dining room.

Color Match Fireplace surround base coat: American Tradition Woodrow Wilson Linen

yellow sienna marble

TOOLS AND MATERIALS

- Latex gloves
- Latex paint, satin, pale creamy yellow
- Paint bucket and grid
- House painter's brush
- Sandpaper (220- to 400-grit)
- Tack cloth
- Medium, composed of 1 part linseed oil and 1 part thinner
- Clean, empty tuna can
- Japan drier

- Artist's oils: titanium white, yellow ochre, raw sienna, burnt sienna, raw umber, ivory black
- Artist's palette
- 3-inch chip brushes
- ⅜-inch round short-haired hog-bristle artist's brushes
- 4-inch paintbrush (optional for softening)
- Spatter stick
- Varnish, satin or semigloss

1 Apply a pale yellow base coat with a house painter's brush and let it dry completely. Lightly sand with sandpaper and wipe with a tack cloth. Pour about 2 tablespoons of the medium into a tuna can and add two drops of japan drier. Squeeze separate portions of white, yellow ochre, raw sienna, and burnt sienna artist's oils onto a palette.

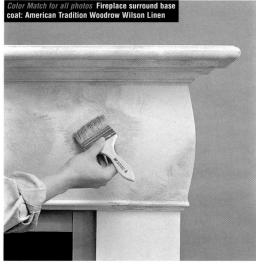

Color Match for all photos Fireplace surround base coat: American Tradition Woodrow Wilson Linen

2 Using a chip brush, pick up a small amount of the medium, then some of each color, and mix loosely on your palette to form a yellow glaze. Lightly brush the glaze onto the surface in a criss-cross fashion. To make some areas lighter and some darker, vary the proportions picked up with the brush. Soften the effect by whisking the same brush over the surface after applying the glaze.

3 While the yellow glaze is still wet, dip a second chip brush into the medium and then into the white artist's oil and brush the result randomly onto some of the lighter portions of the glaze. With the first chip brush, blend in the white paint, creating a cloud-like effect and establishing a directional pattern.

4 Dip a ⅜-inch artist's brush into the medium and then pick up some yellow ochre, raw sienna, and a tiny bit of white. Loosely sketch in veins to outline some lighter and darker yellow areas. Keep the strokes loose and make the effect as natural as possible. Some veins should be thicker than others, and some should form irregular and lozenge shapes. Others should run at opposing angles. No one direction should be dominant.

LOWE'S QUICK TIP
Always dip a brush
in the medium before
dipping it into an
artist's oil.

5 Whisk the first chip brush over the veining to soften the visual effect. If any part of the pattern seems too sharp or harsh, pounce it out with the tips of the bristles. Pounce between some of the veins on the darker areas, then soften those areas slightly.

6 Squeeze a little raw umber and black artist's oils onto the palette; dip the previously used artist's brush into the medium and pick up some of each. Very lightly sketch in more veins, forming an irregular network. Yellow sienna marble is sometimes heavily veined and sometimes hardly veined at all, so you can put in as much veining as you like. Soften with a third chip brush, brushing in the direction of the strongest vein.

7 With another artist's brush, pick up a small amount of medium and some white and yellow ochre artist's oils, and dot the result into some of the shapes to accent them. Clean the brush and do the same with raw sienna and yellow ochre. Add more veins if you wish. Soften the effect with a clean chip brush or with a paintbrush. Complete all of the marbling to this stage before proceeding to Step 8.

8 Dip a clean chip brush into the medium and then into the white artist's oil; mix on the palette. Spatter on the result as described on pages 148–149, concentrating on the lighter parts of the marble. Soften with the first chip brush, whisking it across the area in a crisscross fashion. Spatter again using raw sienna and yellow ochre and concentrating on the darker areas. Soften with the chip brush. If necessary, touch up the base color, the yellow glaze, or the veins. Let the paint dry completely. Varnish the marbled surface.

grid-based patterns

MANY INTRIGUING DECORATIVE FINISHES, FROM FAUX TILES OR BLOCKS TO diamonds, rely on a repeating design. To produce a consistent pattern, such a design is based on a grid marked on the surface. Some simple patterns just require a grid of horizontal and vertical lines. More complex patterns may require some additional calculating before you lay out the grid. Always complete your planning before you lay out the grid. Careful preparation of the grid insures that corners, differing wall proportions, doors, windows, and any irregularities such as sloping floors are accommodated. The methods on these pages apply to painting a wall, but you can easily adapt them to prepare a floor or other surface.

getting started

Before you begin, you'll need a clear design concept. If you choose blocks or diamonds, for example, you need to know their dimensions. Consider other questions as well. Will the motifs be aligned or staggered? How much space do you want around them? How wide will the faux grout lines between blocks be? Will the diamond shapes continue around corners, or be cut off at the wall edges? If you are placing the pattern on just one portion of the wall, such as the dado (the bottom third) or frieze (the top 10 to 12 inches), how will you treat the top or bottom edges?

Getting a repeating pattern of blocks, diamonds, or any other graphic motifs to fit neatly in a given space is a mathematical exercise that may require trial and error. First, plan the size of the basic unit (such as a diamond) and measure its greatest width and height. If you choose a motif centered in an open space, the dimensions of your basic unit must include the space around the motif (see illustration below left). If your pattern will include faux grout lines, include one grout width in each dimension. For instance, if you want to create 12- by 18-inch limestone blocks with ¼-inch grout lines, the grid unit would be 12¼ by 18¼ inches.

For a horizontal repeat, divide the width of the repeating unit into the width of the wall. The result is the number of times the pattern will fit across the wall, plus any fractional excess. When setting up a horizontal repeat on a wall with a door or window opening, it is sometimes best to work from the center of the opening out, so the motif frames it in the most attractive way. For a vertical repeat, divide the height of the repeating unit into the height of the wall (or the distance between baseboard and chair rail or between chair rail and ceiling), excluding baseboard and ceiling mouldings. The result is the number of times the pattern will fit into the space, plus any excess.

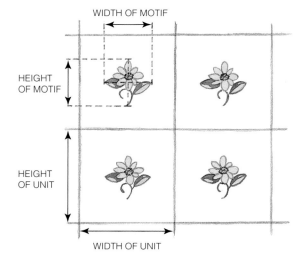

WIDTH OF MOTIF

HEIGHT OF MOTIF

HEIGHT OF UNIT

WIDTH OF UNIT

The excess can be accommodated in one of several ways. You may choose to adjust the size of the overall pattern so it fits exactly in the allotted space. This is easier to do for a diamond pattern than for others, and can be awkward if you make much more of an adjustment in one direction (vertically, for example) than the other. Alternatively, you may be able to adjust any open area around the motif. Another possibility is to make the pattern deliberately unequal—for instance, with a diamond pattern, perhaps the middle and end diamonds could be slightly smaller or larger than the rest. For some patterns, such as blocks, it is acceptable to end on a partial unit. Consider how the pattern will look as it ends or wraps around a corner.

turning a corner

If you'd like a pattern to turn a corner, you need to plan ahead for that, too. Diamonds might straddle a corner. However, faux blocks or tiles should be cut off at corners, regardless of whether the units are complete.

If your pattern is going to turn the corner, it's best to work out the corner treatment before planning how the pattern will repeat on the rest of the wall. If more than one corner is involved and the repeat doesn't fit evenly between them, add a complementary motif on the wall midway or in several places between the two corners, such as a flower between leaves or a moon between stars.

Once you have the pattern planned, you may want to make a scale drawing on graph paper. Or you can go directly to marking it on the wall with chalk or water-soluble lead pencil.

marking the grid

Most tile and block patterns look best if they are centered, so begin by marking the center of each wall. To find it, measure from corner to corner at the ceiling and the floor and at several points in between. Snap a chalk line on the center line from ceiling to floor. Use a plumb bob to make sure the line is plumb; if it isn't, adjust the marks, brush off the first line, and snap again.

Read the following all the way through before beginning.

marking horizontal lines

If your grid extends from the floor to the ceiling, measure and mark the height of one unit (for example, a block or a diamond) above the baseboard all across the wall. Snap a horizontal chalk line and use a level to check that it is level. Measuring up from this line, snap the subsequent horizontal lines onto the wall.

For a grid that covers only part of the wall, first snap the line closest to the middle of the wall—that is, the top edge for a

SNAPPING A CHALK LINE FOR PAINTING

Chalk lines, available in home improvement stores, are small boxes containing 50 to 100 feet of string on a reel and, in many cases, blue chalk. If yours has blue chalk, which is difficult to wipe off, for any painting project you should empty out the box and refill it with a mixture of 3 parts talcum powder and 1 part blue chalk.

To snap a chalk line longer than 3 feet, you can fasten the end of the line with a small nail, but if you prefer not to put even a small hole in your wall, you'll need a partner. (Use three people to snap really long lines.) One person should hold the chalk box on the mark at one end of the desired line while the other stretches the string to the mark at the opposite end and holds it taut. With the chalk line in position, pull the center of the string away from the surface and release it. It will leave a straight, powdery line between the marks. Paint or glaze won't adhere to chalk, so once you've masked the pattern (see page 176), brush or wipe off the chalk line with a clean paper towel. (If you use water-soluble lead pencil instead of chalk, also erase those marks before painting.)

section along the bottom of the wall, or the bottom edge for a section at the top. Check that it is level, and then measure from that line into the patterned area to snap the remaining lines.

marking vertical lines

If your grid is regular, meaning that the centers of the units are aligned vertically (a diamond or checkerboard pattern, for instance), measure and mark the intervals on the wall with water-soluble lead pencil, marking at the ceiling, floor, and several places between. Snap the first vertical line and check that it is plumb. Snap the subsequent lines.

For a staggered grid (limestone blocks, for example, are usually staggered), mark and snap the intervals for the vertical lines. Very lightly pencil in these lines on every other row. Brush off the vertical chalk lines. Starting with half of the interval, mark and snap another set of vertical lines. Lightly pencil in these lines on the rows not already marked, and again brush off the vertical chalk lines (see illustration below).

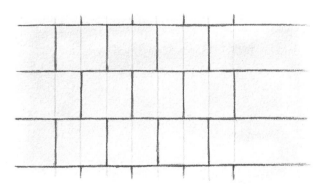

masking the grid

Tape around the units, aiming to paint as many as possible before retaping, but do not try to paint adjacent units that are in different colors.

For a checkerboard pattern, mask all the edges of every other square, positioning the tape inside the squares not to be painted and leaving the chalk lines exposed. Cut the tape so that all the edges are neat.

For a pattern that includes grout lines, apply narrow masking tape to the top and right edges of each unit. (You can find tape in $1/16$- to $1/4$-inch widths at an office or art supply store.) If you are consistent in taping the same sides of each grid unit, the painted units won't vary in size. Once the grid is masked, erase any penciled marks or lines.

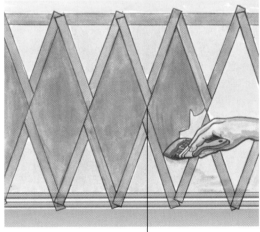

TRIM TAPE OVERLAP

imitating **limestone** blocks

A PATTERN OF FAUX STONE MAY LOOK complicated, but creating one is as simple as marking and taping a grid pattern on the wall, sponging and spattering the block units, and removing the tape. As you'll see, you may not even need to touch up the grout lines.

A standard stone block is twice as long as it is wide, but there is no requirement that all your blocks be identical. You can make the sizes irregular, which will not only look more rustic but will give you some leeway in fitting the pattern on your walls. This project uses beige-tone glazes to create the look of limestone (close-up right, above). However, natural stones can also have a pink, green, blue, yellow, or gray cast, so start by checking paint chips or sample strips to find the basic color you'd like. Then select three consecutive values of that color for your faux stone.

TOOLS AND MATERIALS

- Latex gloves
- 3-inch painter's masking tape
- Latex paint, flat or eggshell, off-white
- Paint bucket, grid, brushes, and roller for base coat
- Chalk line
- Level
- Water-soluble lead pencil
- ¼-inch masking tape
- Translucent color glaze, 3 consecutive values of beige
- Paint tray with liners
- Large sea sponges
- Bucket filled with water
- Veiner or small chip brush
- Artist's acrylic, raw umber (or any dark brown)
- Artist's palette
- Spatter stick
- Touchup brush
- Lightweight straightedge

PROJECT CONTINUES ➡

You can adjust the color of your faux limestone blocks to coordinate with other color cues in your decor. Here, the warm hue of the faux stones blends with the wood tones.

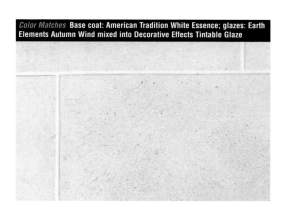

Color Matches Base coat: American Tradition White Essence; glazes: Earth Elements Autumn Wind mixed into Decorative Effects Tintable Glaze

A shadow added along the lines separating the blocks enhances the realistic effect of this faux-stone wall treatment (see Step 8, page 179).

Color Matches Walls: Earth Elements Autumn Wind; glazes: Earth Elements Autumn Wind mixed into Decorative Effects Tintable Glaze

Faux stones on the wall create a rich background for an opulent setting.

1 Mask the areas adjacent to where your faux stone will go. Apply the base coat and let it dry completely.

2 Plan your block size and layout. The blocks shown are 12 by 18 inches with ¼-inch grout lines on a staggered layout. Mark the horizontal courses for the stone blocks by snapping chalk lines (see page 175), making sure to replace any blue chalk with a mix of 3 parts talcum powder to 1 part chalk. If the vertical repeat is such that a very shallow incomplete block course falls below the ceiling, adjust the overall size of the blocks or make the bottom course taller than the others. Then mark the vertical dividing lines with a pencil. Apply narrow tape to the grid, placing the tape consistently in relation to the lines (see page 176). After taping, wipe off any exposed chalk lines and erase pencil marks.

Color Matches **Walls: base coat: Valspar Translucent Cream; glaze: Decorative Effects Translucent Glaze Burnt Sienna; trim: American Tradition Swiss Coffee**

Color Matches **Base coat: American Tradition White Essence; glazes: Earth Elements Autumn Wind mixed into Decorative Effects Tintable Glaze**

LOWE'S QUICK TIP

Most block patterns look best when the bottom course is a full unit deep. If you are painting only a dado—the lower portion of a wall—the course immediately below the top "trim" should also be the full unit depth.

3 Pour some of the darkest beige glaze into a paint tray. (To mix your own glaze, see page 71.) Dip a sponge in the water, wring it out, and dip it into the glaze. Sponge the surface, creating some dense areas, some less dense, and some that are completely open. Let the glaze dry. Repeat with the medium beige glaze, filling in some of the empty areas. If you have trouble keeping track of where you've added the second glaze, stand back and look at your taped grid—the more glaze you add, the less of the tape you'll see.

4 Repeat with the lightest beige glaze, filling in the open areas so that there are definite lighter and darker areas. If you think the overall effect needs greater contrast, sponge on more of any color in selected areas.

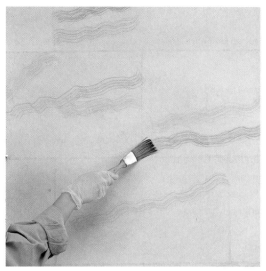

5 Take up some of the medium beige glaze on a veiner or a small chip brush and drag it laterally across the various areas to create wavy veins. Immediately pat with the clean side of the sponge. Make sure each vein starts and stops within or at the edge of a block. (In the photographs shown here, the vein color is exaggerated for clarity.)

6 Place the raw umber artist's acrylic on an artist's palette. Dip the veiner or chip brush in water, then mix the paint to watercolor consistency. Drag on more wavy veins and pat with the sponge as before.

LOWE'S QUICK TIP

When latex paints and glazes are close in value, as these are, it can be hard to tell them apart. Avoid confusion by using a different paint tray for each glaze, labeling them "dark," "medium," and "light."

7 Mix some raw umber on your palette with any one of the beige glazes. Take up some of the paint on the chip brush and spatter it across the stone blocks. You can spatter all over or just in some areas. The more you spatter, the more realistic the effect can be. You can also spatter with all three beige glazes. To add nuance, pounce some of the spatters with the tip of the chip brush; blot other areas with the sponge.

8 Remove the tape. Let the glaze dry completely, and check for any pencil or chalk lines you might have missed. The off-white base coat under the tape will form the grout lines. If you wish, you can create realistic dimension by adding shadow lines to the bottom and right edges of each block. Use a touchup brush to mix raw umber and water to the consistency of watercolor on your palette. Hold a lightweight straightedge tipped at an angle away from the wall as a guide to keep the accent line straight. Let it dry.

painting **diamonds** with a border

A DIAMOND PATTERN LENDS A ROOM an air of sophistication, much as fine wood paneling does. This project places the treatment in the dado or lower third of the wall and tops it with a horizontal border. The diamond shapes are created over a light base coat by applying a glaze in a contrasting color with a pad applicator.

Many variations are possible. You could change the effect by dragging or sponging the background and then painting the diamonds with a brush, for example. Or, to create a very subtle pattern, paint the diamonds the same color as the background, but in a different sheen.

TOOLS AND MATERIALS

- Latex paint, satin
- Paint bucket, grid, brushes, and rollers for base coat
- Painter's masking tape
- 4-foot straightedge
- Water-soluble lead pencil
- Level
- Translucent color glaze
- Paint tray with liners
- 2-inch paintbrush
- Hobby knife
- Pad applicator

1 Apply the base coat and let it dry completely. Tape off any adjacent surfaces you don't wish to paint.

The subtle diamond pattern shown below began with a base coat of lavender pearl finish. The darker diamonds were created with a blue metallic glaze, applied with a felt pad (normally used for edging). Then a warm silver metallic glaze was colorwashed with a felt pad over the entire wall. A warm black, created by mixing two parts of brown with one part of black paint, coats the crown moulding.

Color Match Trim: American Tradition Ebony

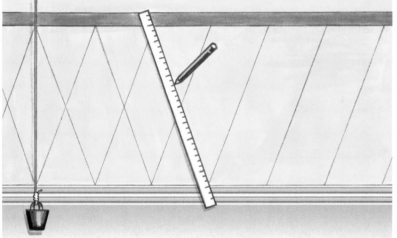

2 Plan your layout, measuring the wall widths and calculating the width of the diamonds so they will fit evenly around the room (see pages 174–176). Starting at the top of the baseboard and measuring up, mark the height of the diamonds at several points along the wall, using a water-soluble lead pencil in a color close to the base coat. Connect these marks, using a straightedge. Use a level to check that the line is level and adjust it if necessary. Draw another line 3 inches above the first to serve as the top of the ornamental border. Measure along the top of the baseboard, starting at one end, and mark half the width of a diamond, to indicate the bottom point of the first diamond. Continue around the room, marking full diamond widths. Repeat along the bottom of the border to mark the tops of the diamonds.

Create the diamonds with diagonal lines. Starting at one top corner, using the straightedge and water-soluble pencil, draw a line to the adjacent bottom mark. Continue marking parallel diagonal lines around the room. Then draw lines from each bottom mark to the adjacent top mark to complete the diamond pattern.

3 Run painter's masking tape along the outside edges of the horizontal border. Pour some of the glaze into a paint tray. (To mix your own glaze, see page 71.) Load a 2-inch paintbrush with the glaze and paint the border. If you wish to paint the baseboard the same color as the border, you can do it at the same time. Remove the tape and let the paint dry completely.

4 Run painter's masking tape along the outside edges of all diamonds (see illustration, page 176); use a hobby knife with a new blade to trim away overlap, forming perfect diamonds. Pour more glaze into the paint tray and use a paintbrush to apply paint to the pad applicator. Carefully dab the paint onto the interior of the diamonds to create a cloud-like effect. When all the diamonds are painted, remove the tape and let the paint dry completely. Wipe off any remaining pencil marks.

Color Match Diamonds base coat: American Tradition Roman Candle

Diamonds dabbed on in Valspar's Breakwater add pattern and texture to transform a plain hallway.

LOWE'S QUICK TIP

If you want to add more graphic elements, use a stencil to add a pattern such as a circle in the border above each diamond. It can be in the same color as the background or in a complementary color.

decorative effects for furnishings and woodwork

USING DECORATIVE PAINT TECHNIQUES, YOU CAN TRANS-
form ordinary cabinets, woodwork, or furniture into focal points
for your decor. Items you consider castoffs may make great candidates for such a treatment—dated plywood cabinets from the
1960s, for example, an old chair found at a garage sale, or even
that coffee table from your first apartment. If you don't have any
old pieces to work on, look for bargains at flea markets, yard
sales, or thrift stores. You can also use unfinished wood furniture
purchased from a retailer.

This chapter shows how to apply finishes ranging from traditional to highly unusual. Once you get comfortable with these
techniques, you can use them on just about any surface. You can
also combine techniques. For instance, try a crackle finish on a
chair and then stencil a small design on top of it. Or drag the
frame of a cabinet and rag the raised panel of the cabinet door.
The key to success is to select color, texture, and pattern for
your project that will complement the overall color scheme of
your room.

The vital first step in restoring both unfinished and old wood
furniture is surface preparation, which is explained on pages
184–185. Once your piece is properly prepped, you're ready to
spread the drop cloth, get out your paints and tools (see pages
76–77 for special decorative painting tools), and start having fun.

Always wear latex gloves for projects that use alkyd finishes or
solvents to protect your hands from harmful chemicals, as well as
hard-to-remove color.

Color Matches on photos, designating paints available at Lowe's, have been provided by Valspar. Due to the limitations of the printing process, colors printed on the pages of this (or any) book may not be an exact representation of a specified paint or specialty product. Check paint chips at Lowe's for the true colors. If you like the color on the page better than the one on the paint chip, a Lowe's Paint Sales Specialist can mix a match for you.

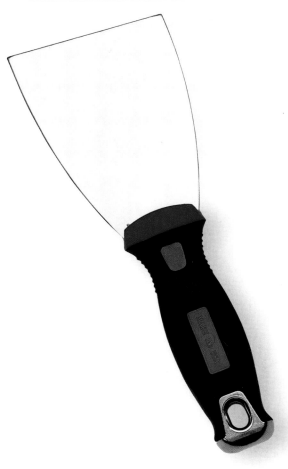

getting started

selecting old furniture

The easiest furniture to refinish is made of solid wood and has smooth surfaces. Avoid veneered pieces if the veneer is buckled or chipped.

All wood furniture should have strong joints and stand square on the floor without wobbling. To check chairs, kneel on the seat while holding onto the chair back and rock gently back and forth to detect loose joints. Minor blemishes such as nicks and scratches can be either repaired or retained to add to the character of the piece, but don't bother with furniture that shows any sign of dry rot or termite damage.

preparing furniture for painting

Unfinished wood requires just a little sanding to remove any blemishes and create a smooth surface.

It is possible to paint over an old piece as long as the surface is in good shape. If the finish has no sheen, clean it with a sponge and mild detergent. Rinse off any soap residue; let the piece dry completely. A glossy finish should be roughed up. Sand it with fine-grit sandpaper or use a liquid deglosser or trisodium phosphate (TSP). Rinse the surface well after using these products and let the surface dry thoroughly. If the cleaning has raised the grain of the wood, lightly sand it with fine-grit sandpaper and wipe it thoroughly with a tack cloth.

removing clear coatings

If you want to reveal the original wood for such projects as distressing or pickling, or if the existing finish is in bad shape, you'll need to strip away the old finish. The existing coating is most likely to be wax, a clear coating, or paint.

To find out which it is, perform a few simple tests. First, soak a cotton ball with turpentine and apply it to an unobtrusive spot. If the coating comes off, it's wax, and you can remove it with turpentine. If the coating doesn't come off, dab on some denatured alcohol, letting it soak in for ten minutes. If the finish dissolves, it is shellac and can be removed with more denatured alcohol. If there is no reaction, brush a small amount of lacquer thinner over the same spot. If the finish dissolves, it is lacquer and can be wiped away with lacquer thinner. If the three tests have no effect, the finish is a varnish or polyurethane and can be removed with a suitable chemical stripper.

stripping paint

Probe peeling paint with a putty knife to see how many layers of accumulated buildup there are. If there's just one layer of paint, scrape it, then sand with fine-grit sandpaper to feather any edges to a smooth finish.

For multiple layers of old paint, chemical strippers are the best choice. Check the labels carefully to find the product that is appropriate for your job. The safest ones do not contain the toxic chemical methylene chloride. Also look for the phrases "no cleanup" or "wash away with water" on the label. The "no cleanup" kind may leave a residue, which must be sanded away. Residue from a "wash away" type can be removed by rinsing with water, but the water may raise the wood grain, so it will need to be lightly sanded. Strippers come as liquids—only good for horizontal sur-

LOWE'S SAFETY TIP

Be wary of any piece that may have been painted before 1978—the old paint may contain lead. This is not a problem if you paint over it. However, if you plan to scrape, sand, or strip the old paint, follow the precautions on page 82.

faces—or in thicker formulations referred to as gels, semipastes, or pastes.

Before you use a stripper, clean off dirt and scrape away loose, peeling, and flaking paint, rounding the corners of your scraping tool to prevent it from gouging the wood. Apply the stripper as directed, and be sure to allow time for it to work, then remove the paint. You may need to apply the stripper more than once, removing more paint each time. If necessary, follow up the chemical stripping by rubbing the wood with medium-grade steel wool. Soaking the steel wool in the stripper may help remove stubborn spots.

Follow the manufacturer's directions for cleaning the stripper residue from the wood. Allow the piece to dry thoroughly.

An alternative to chemical strippers is a heat gun, which softens the paint so that you can scrape it off.

repairing blemishes and sanding

You'll often need to remedy small imperfections as well. Apply a wood filler to damaged areas with your finger and let it dry; apply more than one layer if necessary to achieve a level surface. Sand each layer after it dries. Insert carpenter's glue under any loose veneer.

Sand with 120-grit sandpaper to clean off any remaining finish and to smooth the wood. Then refine the surface with 220-grit sandpaper. Finishing sanders do particularly well at quickly achieving a uniform smoothness. Be careful to sand with the grain. Always clean the dust away with a tack cloth before painting.

Above: Paint scrapes off easily when softened with a chemical paint remover. Always wear rubber gloves when working with these chemicals.

Below: When using an electric finishing sander, apply even pressure as you sweep it across the surface. Too much pressure will gouge the wood.

LOWE'S SAFETY TIP

Chemical strippers soften, peel, and blister paint and varnish; you do not want them to do the same to your skin, lungs, or eyes. Always follow the safety recommendations on the container.

easy embellishments

comb-painting a coffee table

YOU DON'T HAVE TO SPEND A LOT OF money to have a coffee table that looks terrific. A great way to add style is to comb a geometric pattern into the top. This project starts with a dark base coat; then a contrasting color of glaze is applied with a notched squeegee or a rubber paint comb. A "comb" you make yourself out of a plastic container lid or cardboard will approximate this effect. For a more colorful table, use two colors of glaze (see Step 3). The technique shown here will also work well on a raised panel door or on the seat of a solid wood chair.

TOOLS AND MATERIALS

- Wood table
- Wood filler
- Sandpaper (220- to 400-grit)
- Tack cloth
- Wood primer
- Paint tray with liners
- 2- and 4-inch paintbrushes
- Latex paint, satin
- Painter's masking tape
- Translucent color glaze (1 or 2 colors)
- Notched 8-inch squeegee or rubber paint comb
- Water-base polyurethane varnish

Color Matches for all photos Table: base coat: Earth Elements Petrified Wood; glaze: Decorative Effects Translucent Glaze Buff

The combed pattern on this simple wood table is a great complement to rattan and other informal furniture.

Color Match **Wall: Earth Elements Frozen Inlet**

1 Prepare the table as directed on pages 184–185. Seal the wood with primer using a 4-inch paintbrush. Let the primer dry and then apply a base coat of latex paint with a clean paintbrush. Allow this coat to dry completely. Apply painter's masking tape 2 inches in from the table edge, with a crisp miter line at each corner, creating a 2-inch-wide border that you will paint first.

2 Pour some glaze into a lined paint tray. (To mix your own glaze, see page 71.) Use a 2-inch paintbrush to apply glaze to fill the border area. While the glaze is still wet, comb a line of stripes along each side of the border. Remove the tape. Let the glaze dry for at least 4 hours.

You can achieve different patterns on a tabletop depending on what type of graining comb you use. Choose one with smaller teeth for a more delicate textural finish.

3 To create a crisp edge between the two patterns, tape over the edges of the painted border. Use the 4-inch paintbrush to apply glaze to the rectangle inside the tape, using a second color if you wish. Starting at one corner, pull the comb across the paint in one continuous, wavy movement. Repeat until the rectangle is completely covered with a series of wavy lines. While the paint is still wet, comb in the opposite direction. Remove the tape, let the glaze dry thoroughly, and cover the entire tabletop with a water-base polyurethane sealer for protection.

LOWE'S QUICK TIP

Test the wavy motion and pattern on a sheet of cardboard before beginning. You'll become more comfortable with the tool and see how much pressure is needed.

painting a **canvas floorcloth**

IF YOU WANT TO ADD PATTERN TO A floor but don't want to permanently alter it, a painted canvas floorcloth can be a good solution—and it's surprisingly easy to make. Such a floor covering is more durable than it looks and can add as much color and pattern to your room as you want. You can create an original design on the canvas or borrow a design from another source.

This project uses a tracer projector (available at crafts stores for under $100), which can enlarge images up to 14 times. This small machine (see opposite page) projects a decorative pattern onto the canvas, where it can be traced with a pencil. If you have a larger pattern or a smaller canvas—or don't mind moving the projection around the canvas in several steps— you can use a less expensive projector that enlarges an image up to ten times the original.

You can also use stencils or stamps to add pattern over a background color on your floorcloth, or simply paint alternate color blocks across the surface of the mat. Several coats of polyurethane will protect whatever pattern you create.

TOOLS AND MATERIALS

☐ Canvas, medium weight		☐ Painter's masking tape
☐ Primer		☐ Projector
☐ Paint tray with liners		☐ "Cat's tongue" artist's brush
☐ Foam rollers		☐ Artist's acrylic paint, in a second color
☐ Latex paint, satin		
☐ Pattern		
☐ Water-soluble lead pencil		☐ Varnish, matte
		☐ Scissors
		☐ Fabric glue

Above: A painted floor-cloth requires a very small investment in tools and materials.

Right: Using a projector means you don't have to be an artist to make an attractive floorcloth.

Color Matches for all photos (American Tradition colors)
Blue base coat: Bluejay; white base coat: White Peony

1 Start with a sheet of canvas that is larger by 1 inch on all sides than the desired finished rug; the excess allows room for a hem. Prime the canvas and let it dry, then mark for the finished edges, 1 inch in from each side. With a foam roller, apply a coat of latex paint as the background color, covering the entire top side of the canvas. Allow the paint to dry completely. If the paint coverage isn't complete, apply a second coat and let it dry.

2 If you plan to paint your pattern freehand, you can outline it on the canvas with a pencil before applying paint. Otherwise, photocopy your design onto a sheet of white paper. Using painter's masking tape, hang the canvas on a wall in a room that can easily be darkened. Place the projector approximately 8 feet from the wall and project the pattern onto the canvas. Move the projector forward or back until the pattern on the canvas is exactly the desired size. Trace it onto the canvas with a pencil.

3 Take down the canvas and use the "cat's tongue" brush, which has a flat, rounded tip, to paint the pattern using artist's acrylic paint. If you are applying a light color over a dark one, you may have to use two coats. Allow the paint to dry completely.

4 Apply varnish with a foam roller, according to the manufacturer's instructions. Apply at least three coats, allowing the varnish to dry completely between coats. To finish the edges of the canvas, fold under 1 inch on all sides. Use scissors to cut a triangle out of each corner. Adhere the folded-under edges with fabric glue, weighing down the edges while the glue dries.

Two-color designs meld well with almost any design scheme. Use multiple colors and a bold design to create a floorcloth that becomes the focal point of a room (see photo on page 42).

the illusion of age

antiquing a table

AN OLD TABLE CAN BE MADE TO LOOK like a valuable country-style antique with a little elbow grease and a few coats of paint. Pre-existing nicks, cracks, stains, and scratches actually enhance the effect—plus they help to hide any shortcomings in your technique. Make sure you sand off any existing varnish or sealant before priming the table so that the paint will adhere properly.

TOOLS AND MATERIALS

- Wood table
- Wood filler
- Sandpaper (220- to 400-grit)
- Tack cloth
- Wood stain-blocking primer
- Paint tray with liners
- 2-inch paintbrushes
- Latex paint, satin, brown wood color and finish color
- Acrylic varnish, matte

Spruced up with paint and then strategically sanded, a flea-market find has an attractively worn look. The base coat is Valspar's American Tradition Brown Derby; the finish coat is Cranapple.

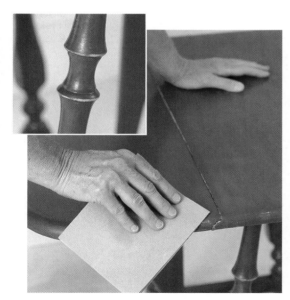

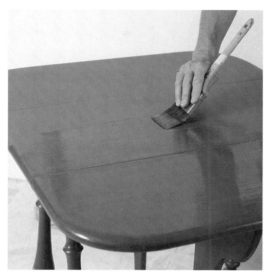

1 Prepare the table as directed on pages 184–185, but remember that some signs of age give the table character, so don't do too much. Seal the wood with the primer, using a paintbrush. Let the primer dry and then apply a base coat of wood-colored latex paint. Allow the paint to dry completely.

2 Using a clean 2-inch paintbrush, apply your chosen finish color of latex paint to the tabletop, underside of the top, and legs, as well as to any cracks or crevices in the wood. Let the paint dry.

3 With 400-grit sandpaper, lightly sand off small areas around the edges and corners of the tabletop and legs. The idea is to imitate natural wear and tear, so sand more from those areas that would be frequently touched or bumped.

4 When the paint is completely dry, brush on two coats of varnish, letting the varnish dry between coats.

LOWE'S QUICK TIP

To add another layer of color, tint the primer and sand through the base coat to let it show.

distressing paneled walls

REAL AGED WOOD BOARDS CAN BE HARD TO find, but the relatively easy finishing technique shown here allows you to make an unblemished new surface look anything from mildly worn to truly beaten up. The more layers of paint you apply, the more aged the wood will appear. Sanding away areas of a single layer of paint may provide the look you're after. Or you can work with several different values of one color, as in the project shown here—the base coat is light blue, the glaze is ultramarine blue, and the spattering is dark blue. The spattering adds more depth and interest to the finish.

Below: **Distressed-wood wainscot and cabinet doors combine with a lime-washed wall for the effect of an old room that has aged well.**

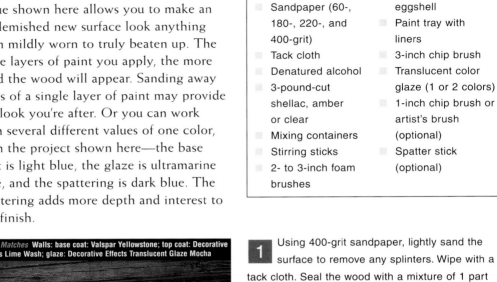

Color Matches Walls: base coat: Valspar Yellowstone; top coat: Decorative Effects Lime Wash; glaze: Decorative Effects Translucent Glaze Mocha

TOOLS AND MATERIALS

- Latex gloves
- Sandpaper (60-, 180-, 220-, and 400-grit)
- Tack cloth
- Denatured alcohol
- 3-pound-cut shellac, amber or clear
- Mixing containers
- Stirring sticks
- 2- to 3-inch foam brushes
- Latex paint, flat or eggshell
- Paint tray with liners
- 3-inch chip brush
- Translucent color glaze (1 or 2 colors)
- 1-inch chip brush or artist's brush (optional)
- Spatter stick (optional)

1 Using 400-grit sandpaper, lightly sand the surface to remove any splinters. Wipe with a tack cloth. Seal the wood with a mixture of 1 part denatured alcohol and 1 part 3-pound-cut shellac, applied with a foam brush. This will keep the wood from absorbing paint. Let the shellac dry. Lightly sand the surface and wipe with the tack cloth.

2 Apply the latex base coat to the wood with the 3-inch chip brush; don't worry if the coverage is not even. Let the paint dry completely. Sand the entire surface lightly and irregularly—removing more paint in some areas, less in others—using 180- or 220-grit sandpaper; experiment with different grades of sandpaper to see which effect you like best.

Right: **A dark blue glaze spattered over a lighter blue gives an attractive illusion of wear.**

Color Matches Base coat: Earth Elements Crystal Falls; glaze: Decorative Effects Translucent Glaze Bluebell

3 Pour some glaze into lined paint tray. (To mix your own glaze, see page 71.) With the 3-inch chip brush, streak the glaze unevenly over the surface, brushing loosely but always in the direction of the wood grain. If the surface has multiple components, such as rails and stiles, be sure to follow the grain direction of each one. At this point, the distressing effect will be soft, rather than rustic. You can stop now if you are pleased with the balance of colors and exposed wood.

4 For a more rustic look, lightly sand the surface using 60-grit sandpaper. Sand away more color from selected areas and feather the edges of the different layers. Wipe the surface with the tack cloth. If you want more color, apply another coat of glaze and then sand again.

5 With a clean foam brush, apply another coat of the alcohol-shellac mixture and let it dry. Lightly sand the surface with 220-grit sandpaper to dull the sheen, but be careful not to sand through the previous layers. Wipe the surface clean with the tack cloth.

6 If you would like to accent the surface with spatters of color, mix an accent glaze of a darker color in a small container. Spatter it on with a 1-inch chip brush or artist's brush (see pages 148–149). Try to create random patterns rather than a uniform haze.

pickling woodwork

PICKLING WOOD PANELS, TRIM, FLOORS, or cabinetry is a simple process that involves lightly staining the wood with a colored glaze. Unlike distressing wood, it doesn't require extensive sanding, and it leaves an even finish that allows the grain of the wood to show through the glaze color. Pickling is often used on floors and paneling to impart a sense of country style, and it works well in any informal decor.

An off-white glaze, as shown here, is the most popular choice for pickling, but you can use any pastel color that comple-ments your wall color. If you are pickling a large, unbroken surface, choose an alkyd glaze to show fewer brush strokes. If you are pickling furniture, apply an appropriate protective finish after the final step.

TOOLS AND MATERIALS

- Latex gloves
- Sandpaper (220-grit)
- Tack cloth
- Translucent color glaze
- Paint tray with liners
- 3-inch foam brush
- Paper towels

These wooden shutters, a hallmark of early American homes, have been pickled and lightly distressed (see pages 192–193) to give an authentic look to this rustic-style room. It's a beautiful treatment with the pale colorwashed walls and rough-hewn beams.

Color Matches Wall: base coat: American Tradition White; glaze: Decorative Effects Translucent Glaze Maize; window and shutters: Decorative Effects Translucent Glaze White

Color Match for all photos **Glaze: Decorative Effects Translucent Glaze White**

1 Sand the surface to remove any splinters and roughness. Wipe with a tack cloth. Pour some glaze into a lined paint tray. (To mix your own glaze, see page 71.) Apply the glaze with a foam brush, brushing in the direction of the wood grain. If the surface has multiple components, such as rails and stiles, be sure to follow the grain direction of each one. Work on one component, such as a board or a rail, at a time, and stop at natural seams.

2 Immediately wipe off the glaze, using a folded or wadded paper towel; wipe in the direction of the wood grain.

3 Assess the results so far. At this point the natural wood grain pattern should show quite clearly through the light glaze, although the effect will vary with the type of wood and glaze color. You can stop at this stage if you are pleased with the balance of color and wood grain.

4 For an effect with more color and less wood grain, apply a second coat of glaze and wipe it as before. With a second coat, the glaze will be more opaque.

milk-painting a bureau

THE DISTRESSING TECHNIQUE SHOWN here involves two colors of milk paint (see page 62) that are different values of the same color (see page 10), sealed with a final layer of beeswax. Milk paint is available at craft and antique stores and over the Internet. You can use it on unfinished wood, as in this example, or over a previously painted surface. Just make sure to scrub a previously painted surface with trisodium phosphate (see page 82) and lightly sand it before you start.

TOOLS AND MATERIALS

- Wood bureau
- Wood filler
- Sandpaper (150-grit)
- Tack cloth
- Milk paint (2 colors)
- Mixing container
- Stirring stick
- Cheesecloth
- 2- to 3-inch paintbrush
- Clean rag
- Beeswax

Milk paint comes in a range of colors, reflective of early Colonial and Shaker paint that was made from earth pigments. Like the milk paint used centuries ago, the colors you buy today won't fade. If you leave the finish as is rather than sand it, there will be subtle differences of shading.

1 Remove the drawers from the bureau and any knobs or handles from the drawers. Prepare the bureau as directed on pages 184–185. Mix the first milk paint with water according to the manufacturer's directions. Try not to mix more than you will need, as milk paint has a limited shelf life. Strain the paint through cheesecloth to remove any lumps. Brush the paint on all visible surfaces of the bureau and the drawer fronts. Let it dry.

2 The paint will soak quickly into a soft, unfinished wood; you may need to apply several coats for uniform coverage. However, the paint dries quickly. Lightly sand between coats to smooth the surface.

4 Using a rag, apply beeswax in a circular motion, working it into the wood.

3 Mix and apply the second color of milk paint and let it dry. Sand through selected areas of the top coat to reveal the first coat of paint, or even the wood, choosing those areas that would naturally be touched frequently, such as around the knobs, on the edges of the drawers, and at the corners.

A Federal blue forms the top coat on this bureau. The lighter base coat was created by mixing the Federal blue with white.

imitating wood grains

ONCE YOU DEVELOP THE SKILL TO create one, a wood-grain faux finish can be realistic enough to make inexpensive plywood or fiberboard hard to distinguish from high-end solid wood. Unlike many decorative painting techniques, wood-graining requires a fair amount of practice to do well. You'll also need to become familiar with the grain characteristics of specific wood species. If you know what the real wood looks like, you can make subtle adjustments as you work to bring out realistic pattern and color.

The next nine pages present techniques for creating three different wood-grain effects. Flogging, the simplest, is generally used as a background to create pores for wood graining, but it can be used alone to create a texture somewhat like bark or shagreen (sharkskin). The technique for duplicating mahogany is more complex, but because you work with wet glaze, wiping off portions to reveal the characteristic vein patterns, you can brush out mistakes as you go along. Imitating pine, a popular wood choice for casual styles, involves painting veins one at a time onto a dry background. You will need to develop good brush control to do that effectively.

Color Match **Decorative Effects Metal and Patina Glaze Bronze**

Above: All is faux above the tiles in this relaxing bathroom. Moulding applied to drywall creates wall panels. The entire wall was primed and then colorwashed with a dry brush and transparent bronze glaze to replicate wood grain.

Right: The graining on this door is a fantasy interpretation of exotic woods, using several different techniques including knotty pine (see pages 204–207). The door frame is an imaginary stone created with marbling and sponging (see pages 170–173 and 155–157).

Color Match **Wall: American Tradition Rococo Yellow**

flogging

FLOGGING, WHICH CREATES A SMALL-scale pattern that replicates wood pores, can be used with other graining techniques or alone for a subtle texture. To flog, you repeatedly slap the flat side of a special long-bristled brush called a flogger onto wet glaze.

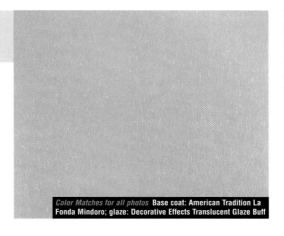

Color Matches for all photos **Base coat: American Tradition La Fonda Mindoro; glaze: Decorative Effects Translucent Glaze Buff**

Notice the evenness of the flogging pattern on this finished panel. You should not see any space between the brush impressions.

1 Prepare the surface as directed on pages 80–87 or 184–185. Apply the base coat and let it dry completely. Mask any areas adjacent to where you'll be working. If you're working on a door or separate panel rather than on a wall, set it against a wall, with two small blocks under the bottom edge and a wedge between the top edge and the wall. Pour some glaze into lined paint tray. (To mix your own glaze, see page 71.) Cut in the first corner of the area to be flogged, using a foam brush. Roll one or two roller widths of glaze from top to bottom, reloading as needed. Hold the flogger parallel to the surface with the bristles straight up. Starting at the bottom corner, slap the bristles onto the surface, moving continuously up the surface in quick successive motions and putting the most pressure at the brush's ferrule. The impressions should overlap slightly.

2 Clean your brush on a rag when it becomes loaded with paint. Once you reach the top, return to the bottom and repeat the process, positioning the brush so the splayed bristles slightly overlap the previous pass. Do not flog the wet edge. Continue applying glaze and flogging it.

TOOLS AND MATERIALS

Latex gloves	Translucent color
Latex paint, satin	glaze
Paint bucket, grid,	Paint tray with
brushes, and roller	liners
for base coat	2-inch foam brush
Painter's	3-inch flogger
masking tape	Clean rag

replicating heart-grain mahogany

MAHOGANY IS PRIZED FOR ITS DEEP red color, distinctive grain, and smooth patina. Once the preferred hardwood for fine furniture and cabinetry, it is now a threatened tree species that is used sparingly. This project provides an inexpensive way to enjoy the rich sophistication of mahogany without adding to its endangerment. Heart-grain mahogany has an arched grain formed by light and dark tones. The key to creating a realistic mahogany faux finish is to start with a base color that matches the lightest tones in the wood you are imitating. While you can work from our photos, the end result will be most realistic if you get a sample board of stained mahogany from a hardwood supplier so you can match the color and study the grain patterns.

LOWE'S QUICK TIP

Prepare the medium in small batches and mix more as you need it.

TOOLS AND MATERIALS

- Latex gloves
- Alkyd paint, satin, peachy orange
- Paint bucket, grid, brushes, and roller for base coat
- Sandpaper (220- to 400-grit)
- Tack cloth
- Painter's masking tape
- Flogging glaze, composed of 1 part raw umber artist's acrylic,1 part Payne's gray artist's acrylic, 2 parts acrylic medium, 1 to 2 parts water
- Mixing containers
- Stirring sticks
- 6-inch roller
- 3-inch flogger
- Denatured alcohol
- 3-pound-cut shellac
- 3-inch foam brush
- Sketch paper
- Carpenter's pencil

- Artist's oils: burnt sienna, burnt umber, alizarin crimson
- Artist's palette
- Medium #1, composed of 1 part linseed oil, 2 parts thinner, japan drier (added later)
- Empty, clean tuna cans
- 3-inch chip brushes
- Burlap scrap
- Paper towels
- ½-inch short-bristled artist's brush
- 2- to 3-inch softening brush
- 2-inch fan brush or veiner
- Medium #2, composed of 1 part linseed oil, 1 part thinner, japan drier (added later)
- Varnish, low luster or semigloss

Color Match **Wall: American Tradition Pink Inspiration**

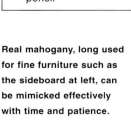

Real mahogany, long used for fine furniture such as the sideboard at left, can be mimicked effectively with time and patience.

1 Prepare the surface as directed on pages 184–185. Apply the base coat and let it dry completely. Lightly sand the paint, and wipe with a tack cloth. Mask the area adjacent to where you'll begin. Mix the flogging glaze and apply it with the roller. Then, using the flogger, flog the exposed surface (see page 199). Always flog in the direction of the grain; turn the brush 90 degrees and flog crosswise for any horizontal components. Repeat as needed until the surface is covered with small "pores." Let it dry.

2 To seal the flogged surface, mix equal parts of denatured alcohol and 3-pound-cut shellac; apply the mixture with a foam brush. Let it dry. Next, cut pieces of sketch paper of roughly the same proportions as each area to be grained. You'll need a different pattern for each principal section. Narrow sections, such as rails and stiles, can have simple straight graining, for which no pattern is necessary. Sketch a graining pattern on each piece of paper (see photo for an example, or use a piece of mahogany as a model).

The finished panel has the richness and depth of genuine mahogany.

3 Squeeze a small amount of each artist's oil onto a palette. Pour 6 tablespoons of medium #1 into a tuna can and add 4 drops of japan drier. Dip a chip brush into the medium and then pick up a little of each color, using more brown or red as you like. Brush on the glaze with crisscross strokes, then drag the brush over the surface in the direction of the grain (see pages 150–151 for dragging).

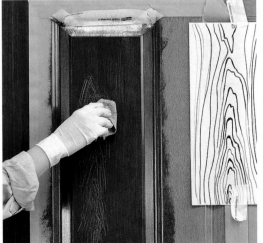

4 Skip this step for any recesses in a raised panel; the dragged lines can be left alone in those areas. Scrunch up a burlap scrap; pinch it between your fingers. Starting at the bottom, use it to roughly draw in only the peaks of the heart-grain portion of your pattern. Round the apexes slightly and avoid making them perfectly symmetrical or aligned. The lines will be very sketchy.

PROJECT CONTINUES ➡

5 With the burlap, extend the sides of each peak toward the bottom. Work from the lowest peak up; be careful not to let the pattern grow progressively wider. Drag the burlap from top to bottom alongside the heart grain to form the side grain. Working away from the heart grain, repeat, gradually straightening the lines.

6 Wrap a tack cloth or paper towel around your thumb and trace over some of the sketched peaks to refine them. Move your thumb up and down in a squiggly motion to add depth as well as width to these highlights.

7 Crush the cloth or paper towel between your fingers. Start at the top of a sketched vein of side grain and wipe all the way to its end, removing a little of the glaze. Repeat all over the glazed surface. Allow the cloth to trail off rather than lifting it partway down.

8 Dip a short-bristled brush into the medium. Pick up some of each artist's oil to create a new, slightly darker color. Paint in some darker accents above the peak highlights. Whisk the brush in short up-and-down strokes to add depth as well as width to these accents. Soften the heart grain by lightly stroking with the chip brush from the open end toward the peak. If your design has peaks pointing up and down, stroke from the bottom up and then from the top down. Following the vein direction, soften the side grain.

9 Dip the short-bristled brush into the medium and pick up some of each artist's oil, mixing in more of the burnt umber than the other colors. The resulting glaze should be transparent enough to add just a haze of color. Starting at the top, draw in accent veins on the side graining. Soften all over using the chip brush or a softening brush. Hold a fan brush or veiner at an angle and, starting at the top, drag it down the side graining as shown here to sharpen some of the veining and break up any thick, dark lines of paint.

10 Soften with the softening brush. To darken the veins, sweep the brush in horizontal strokes; to lighten them, sweep in vertical strokes. Remove any tape at this point and let the graining dry overnight. Clean all the equipment. If there are other areas of your item to be grained, take each to this stage before proceeding.

11 Squeeze a small amount of each artist's oil onto your palette. Measure 6 tablespoons of medium #2 into a tuna can and add 3 to 4 drops of japan drier. Dip a clean chip brush into the medium and then pick up some of each color. This glaze should be transparent enough to add just a haze of color; add more red or brown if you wish. Brush the entire surface with top-to-bottom strokes. Soften with the same brush. With a paper towel, wipe the glaze away from some parts of the pattern to bring out highlights.

12 Holding a chip brush at a 45-degree angle to the surface and using a series of short, interrupted strokes, pull the brush down through the glaze on part of the side grain, creating a ladder pattern of dark undulations. Then soften with the same brush.

13 To create cross pores, hold the same chip brush sideways and press the middle part of the bristles onto darker areas where there are no undulations. Take each area of your item to this stage before proceeding. Let the finish dry. Varnish the grained surfaces to intensify the color and sheen and to protect the paint.

simulating knotty pine

THE VEINS IN KNOTTY PINE ARE DARKER than the background, which means you will paint them freehand onto your panel before applying a thin glaze over your finished work. Typically, a panel will have only one or two knots. The following directions begin with painting a row of peaks for the heart grain and then painting the knots with their surrounding veins, but it doesn't matter which order you do them in.

Pine grain sometimes has a dark area, especially around knots. If you wish to add this feature, stop after you seal the wood in Step 9. Make a wash of equal parts of artist's acrylic and acrylic satin medium. You can vary the color; one good mixture is equal parts of raw and burnt sienna. Blend in an amount of gel retarder equal to no more than 20 percent of the mixture. Brush this wash over the area you wish to darken and let it dry, then complete Step 9.

TOOLS AND MATERIALS

- Latex gloves
- Latex paint, satin, creamy yellow
- Paint bucket, grid, brushes, and roller for base coat
- Sandpaper (220- to 400-grit)
- Tack cloth
- Sketch paper
- Carpenter's pencil
- Artist's tube acrylics: titanium white, raw sienna, burnt sienna
- Artist's palette
- Gel retarder
- Palette knife
- Medium #1, composed of acrylic satin medium and a small amount of gel retarder (see Step 2)
- ½-inch short-bristled artist's brush
- 3-inch chip brushes
- Script liner brush
- Veiner
- Curved painter's tool with comb edge
- Denatured alcohol
- 3-pound-cut shellac, amber
- Mixing containers
- Stirring sticks
- Foam brush
- Medium #2, composed of 1 part linseed oil, 1 part thinner, and japan drier (added later)
- Empty, clean tuna can
- Artist's oils: yellow ochre, raw sienna, burnt sienna
- 3-inch paintbrush or softening brush
- Paper towels
- Varnish, low luster or semigloss

A finished knotty pine panel is almost impossible to distinguish from the real thing.

Color Match for all photos **Base coat: American Tradition Hepplewhite Cream**

LOWE'S QUICK TIP

You can wipe off a painted line at any time. Wrap a paper towel around your finger and rub off the portion you don't like. If the paint has dried, just rub harder.

1 Prepare the surface as directed on pages 184–185. Apply the base coat and let it dry completely. Lightly sand and then wipe with a tack cloth. Next, cut pieces of paper of roughly the same proportions as each area to be grained. You'll need a graining pattern for each principal section. Narrow sections such as rails and styles can either have simple straight graining, for which no pattern is necessary, or can be figured, like the left stile above. Sketch a graining pattern on each piece of paper (see photo for an example or use a piece of pine as a model).

2 Squeeze out a small amount of each of the artist's tube acrylics onto a palette. Place a drop of gel retarder on top of each color. With a palette knife, mix the colors together. Make Medium #1 by placing a tablespoon of acrylic satin medium on your palette and blending it with a drop of retarder. Dip a short-bristled brush into the medium and then pick up some of the mixed paint; blend the two on the palette. Begin drawing the peaks of the heart grain, working from the bottom up for peaks that point up and top down for peaks that point down; use a sketchy motion to add depth as well as width at the top of each peak. If the glaze is too thick, add a drop of water. After you've drawn a few peaks, soften them with a chip brush, starting at the bottom and working upward. This acrylic glaze will dry quickly, so you need to soften your work promptly and often.

LOWE'S SAFETY TIP

Spread out oil-soaked rags to dry outdoors or in a well-ventilated area away from pets, children, sparks, and other sources of combustion; do not leave the materials unattended overnight. Dispose of the materials according to local ordinances.

3 Load the short-bristled brush as before and, working from the lowest peak up, extend the sides of each peak toward the bottom. Keep a little space between the veins, but don't let the pattern grow progressively wider as it works downward.

4 Refer to your sketch and, if there are knots, determine where their centers will fall. With a script liner, paint a small irregular oval for each knot center. Paint in a delicate peaked vein above the knot and then another below the knot, connecting the two. Add another peaked vein above the knot.

PROJECT CONTINUES ➡

5 Continue as in Step 4 to make concentric veins around the knot.

6 Change to the short-bristled brush and add more veins above and then below the knot, sketching in the peaks as before. Soften vertically with a chip brush, moving the brush up or down from the center of the knot. Referring to Step 3 and your sketch, complete this section of heart grain. Mask any adjacent areas before continuing.

7 With a veiner, pick up some of the mixed acrylic paint on your palette along with some acrylic medium. Use the comb edge of a painter's tool to separate the bristles of the veiner. If the paint seems too thick, dip the veiner in water and rub it on the palette.

8 Starting at the top, lightly drag the veiner next to the heart grain patterns to create side grain. If you are graining a panel, rotate your wrist as you drag the sides so the veins fall on the moulding as well as the recess. Rotate your wrist as you fill narrow areas—this will compress the bristles and make the veins closer and denser. Repeat to fill in as necessary. Then let the graining dry. Remove any tape. If other areas of your item need to be grained, take each to this stage before proceeding. Clean all your equipment.

9 Seal the surface with a mixture of equal parts of denatured alcohol and 3-pound-cut shellac, applied with a foam brush. Let it dry. Pour 3 tablespoons of Medium #2 into a tuna can. Add 3 drops of japan drier. Squeeze a small amount of each artist's oil onto your palette. Dip a clean chip brush into the medium and then pick up some of each color paint and apply it to the surface with straight top-to-bottom strokes. The glaze should be transparent, adding just a haze of color. Soften with a 3-inch paintbrush or softening brush. To create highlights, remove the glaze between some veins in the heart grain with a wadded paper towel.

10 Soften again with the paintbrush or softening brush. Wipe off a small dot on each side of the knot. Place the 3-inch paintbrush above each knot and drag it toward the knot, forming a "smile" in the glaze. Drag a "frown" up from below the knot. (The frown is in progress in the photo.) Then soften with the same brush.

11 Hold a clean chip brush at a 45-degree angle to the surface. With short, interrupted strokes, pull the brush down through the glaze on part of the side grain, creating a ladder pattern of dark undulations. Soften with the same brush.

12 To create cross pores, hold the chip brush sideways and press the middle part of the bristles onto areas where there are no undulations. Let the paint dry. If there are other areas of your item to be grained, take all of them to this stage. With the wood-graining complete, varnish the surface to intensify the color and protect the painting, using a tinted or clear varnish, as you wish.

elegant fakes

malachite

Faux malachite adds a refined detail to this black panel door.

MALACHITE, A SEMIPRECIOUS STONE with a distinctive dark green color and swirling pattern, evokes an Art Deco feeling. As a faux finish, malachite should be used on items that would normally be made of stone, such as columns, fireplace surrounds, boxes, or even lamp bases. In a contemporary setting, where things don't have to be what they appear, it can also decorate a door or wall panel. Surprisingly, malachite is fairly easy to imitate. You use a combing technique, dragging a piece of torn cardboard through a wet glaze in curved, wavy lines. Since real malachite is used in small pieces, you will need a design of straight-edged sections, each of which will be patterned individually (see Step 1). The project will take some time; at the end of each day, clean up and prepare additional medium and paint as needed.

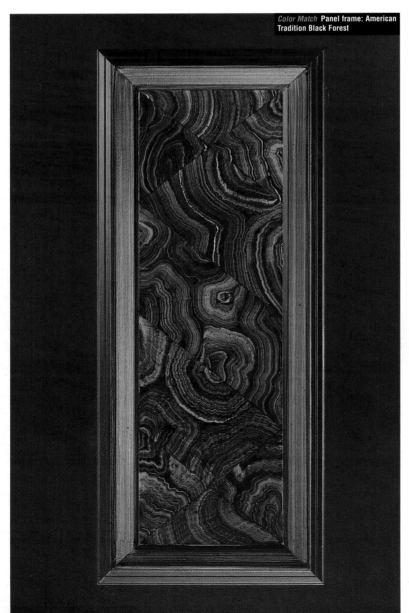

Color Match **Panel frame: American Tradition Black Forest**

TOOLS AND MATERIALS

- Latex gloves
- Acrylic latex primer
- Latex paint, satin, pale blue-green
- Paint bucket, grid, brushes, and roller for primer and base coat
- Sandpaper (220- to 400-grit)
- Tack cloth
- Sketch paper
- Water-soluble lead pencil
- Painter's masking tape
- Scissors or hobby knife
- Shiny, lightweight cardboard
- Medium, com-
- posed of 1 tablespoon linseed oil, 1 tablespoon thinner, 2 drops japan drier
- Empty, clean tuna can
- Artist's oils: indigo blue, cadmium deep green, ivory black
- Artist's palette
- 1½-inch foam brush or artist's brush
- Touchup brush
- Pencil with eraser or eraser tool
- Chip brushes
- Spatter stick
- Varnish, low luster or satin

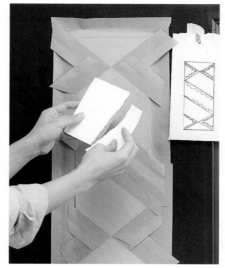
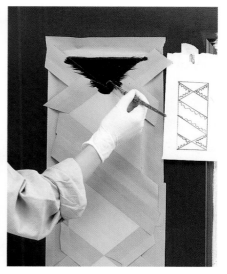

1 Prepare the surface as directed on pages 80–87 or 184–185. Apply the base coat and let it dry completely. If you are applying the malachite finish to just one area, prime and then apply the base coat to the adjacent areas and let them dry. Lightly sand the malachite area and wipe it with a tack cloth. Next, cut a piece of paper of roughly the same proportions as your surface and sketch your design on it. You can paint as many nonadjacent sections at one time as you wish; sections that adjoin them are masked off. After the painted sections dry, you'll mask them off and paint the remaining ones. Therefore, try to set up a pattern in which every other section can be masked at one time. Mark your sketch to indicate the first masking. Draw the design on your surface; apply masking according to your plan, using scissors or a hobby knife to cut the tape to conform to the marked design if necessary. Press the tape firmly to prevent seepage.

2 Tear a small piece of cardboard to use as a painting tool. Don't try to make a clean tear; you need a rough edge for your tool. As you work, you can tear the cardboard further or make other pieces if the first one gets too flimsy.

3 Mix the medium in a tuna can. Squeeze a small amount of each of the artist's oils onto a palette. Dip a foam brush or an artist's brush into the medium and then pick up equal amounts of the colors; mix them on your palette. Brush the resulting glaze onto an exposed section of your surface. If some sections meet point to point (as in this example) it's hard not to apply glaze to both; if that happens, spread the glaze completely over each.

PROJECT CONTINUES ➡

Malachite surrounds the marbled gameboard on this round wood tabletop.

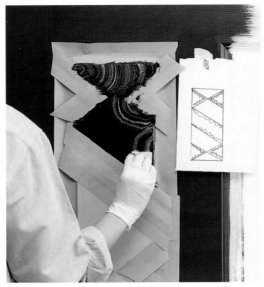

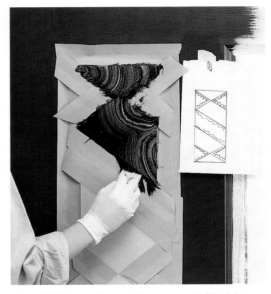

4 Holding the rough edge of the cardboard down (it doesn't matter whether the shiny or dull side faces up), gently drag it over one section in a wavy or circular pattern, ending on the tape. Wiggle the cardboard to make wavering lines. If you don't like the pattern, brush out the glaze and try again.

5 Lift the cardboard. If you haven't filled the section with the malachite pattern, drag another pattern adjacent to the first. You can echo or extend the first pattern, or intersect it with another shape, but don't overlap it. All of the glaze should be patterned, with only the smallest gaps untouched by the cardboard.

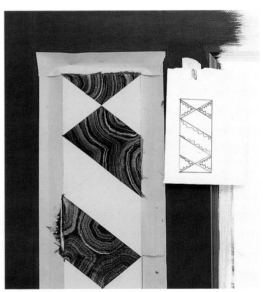

6 To make adjustments to any areas where you think you've removed too much glaze, use a touchup brush dipped into the medium and then into the oils. To lighten an area, drag the edge of a pencil eraser or an eraser tool through the glaze. Move the tool carefully between the dragged lines and try to echo their finesse.

7 After all the exposed sections have been painted, remove the tape and let the paint dry overnight.

8 Mask the next sections to be painted. Repeat steps 3 through 7, and continue in this way until the entire design has been painted. When all the sections have been painted, remove the tape and fill in any gaps between the sections with a touchup brush dipped in the medium and the artist's oils. Let the paint dry.

9 Re-mask the areas that will not be patterned. Dip a chip brush into the medium, then into the artist's oils; gently spatter the glaze over the design. Lightly whisk a dry chip brush all over the surface to soften the effect. Remove the tape. Varnish the surface and let it dry. Finish painting the surrounding areas as needed, masking the malachite finish first.

Color Match **Wall: American Tradition White**

Silvered moulding is a sophisticated complement to the intricacies of the malachite patterning on this obelisk.

tortoiseshell

TOOLS AND MATERIALS

- Latex gloves
- Acrylic latex primer
- Latex paint, semigloss, creamy yellow
- Paint bucket, grid, brushes, and roller for primer and base coat
- Sandpaper (220- to 400-grit)
- Tack cloth
- ⅛-inch masking tape
- Painter's masking tape
- Medium, composed of 1 tablespoon linseed oil, 1 tablespoon
- thinner, 2 drops japan drier
- Empty, clean tuna can
- Artist's oils: burnt sienna, burnt umber, ivory black, asphaltum (if unavailable, use burnt umber)
- Artist's palette
- ½-inch flat artist's brush or paper towel
- ⅜-inch round synthetic sable artist's brush
- 2-inch chip brush
- Foam brush
- Touchup brush
- Varnish, satin to semigloss

TORTOISESHELL HAS A WARM BROWN and black pattern that complements a neutral decor. Use it on a picture frame, wood box, or small tabletop. Since real tortoiseshell was rare and only small pieces were used, your design should be made of small sections, perhaps inset in a plain panel, or used in a checkerboard pattern with alternating blocks of solid color. In this project, the pattern includes a faux ivory inlay that separates the "pieces" of tortoiseshell. If you prefer, you can omit this effect by eliminating the ⅛-inch masking tape and allowing the sections to touch. As with any project involving artist's oils, clean up at the end of each day and prepare medium and paint as needed.

Color Match **Panel frame: American Tradition Black Forest**

Above: A single panel of faux tortoiseshell gives a touch of elegance to a plain black cabinet door.

Right: Faux tortoiseshell frames this mirror.

Color Match **Wall: American Tradition Woodlawn Lace**

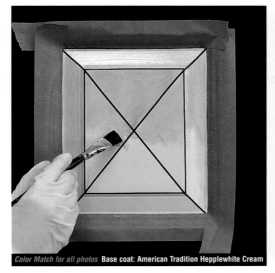

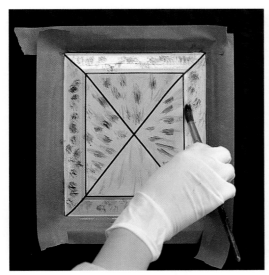

Color Match for all photos **Base coat: American Tradition Hepplewhite Cream**

1 Prepare the surface as directed on pages 184–185. Apply the base coat and let it dry. If your tortoiseshell is an inset, also prime and apply base coat to the adjacent areas and let them dry. Lightly sand the tortoiseshell area and wipe it with a tack cloth. Mark the inlay design, if you are using one, and mask it with ⅛-inch tape. (In this project, the diagonally crossed lines and the edge of the central panel are masked.) If appropriate, mask edges adjacent to the area you'll be painting.

2 Mix the medium in a tuna can. Squeeze small amounts of burnt sienna, burnt umber, and black artist's oils onto a palette. Dip a ½-inch flat artist's brush or a wadded-up piece of paper towel into the medium, then into the burnt sienna, and brush or rub it over the entire surface.

3 Dip a ⅜-inch round artist's brush into the medium, then into the burnt sienna. Dab on the glaze with the side of the brush; all the dabs within a section should point in the same direction, but don't make them uniform. Place dabs closer together in some areas than in others. For a more realistic effect, have some dabs run off the edges of each section, but not into other sections.

4 Dip the ⅜-inch round artist's brush into the medium, then into the burnt umber. Dab on glaze either directly adjacent to or slightly overlapping the burnt sienna markings.

5 With the same brush, repeat the previous step, but using black artist's oil. You can intensify the mottled effect by smearing the black paint slightly. The more mottled areas should be more densely covered with dabs of glaze.

PROJECT CONTINUES ➡

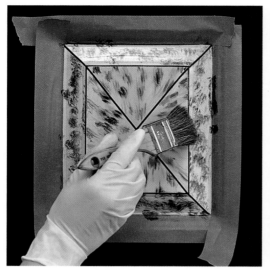

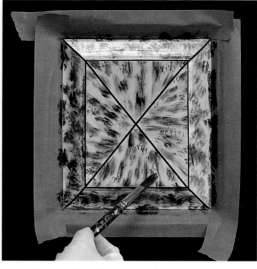

6 Soften the effect by lightly stroking a chip brush over the surface in the direction the dabs point. At this point you can also add more of any of the three colors. Soften with the chip brush after you apply them.

7 Dip the ⅜-inch round artist's brush into the medium and then into the burnt sienna. Dab on tiny specks of color throughout. Then soften again with the chip brush. Remove the tape, touch up any seepage, and let the paint dry overnight.

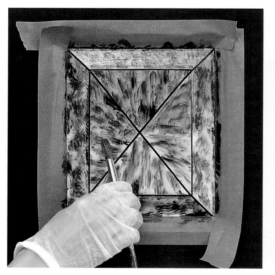

8 Re-mask the design. Squeeze some asphaltum or burnt umber artist's oil onto the palette. Dip the round brush (a foam brush or chip brush will also work) into the medium, then into the paint, and combine them on the palette to make a thin wash. Paint the surface with this wash.

9 If you wish, add more black dots using a touchup brush. Soften with the chip brush. Remove the tape and touch up if necessary. Let the paint dry overnight. Re-mask and then apply the varnish. Finish painting the surrounding area, being sure to mask off the tortoiseshell finish.

gilding

GILDED TRIM—COLUMNS AND OTHER decorative architectural elements such as ceiling medallions or wooden onlays—is common in neoclassical styles. You can either gild full surfaces or run a line of gilt—in an inset section of a moulded trim or around the capital of a column, for example.

There are numerous products you can use to add a metal finish, including paint, powder, and cream mediums. Leafing, the method shown here, can produce some of the prettiest effects, with tiny irregular ridges where the leaves overlap. Leaf should always be applied over a painted surface. You can apply leaf to a flat or a moulded surface, covering it entirely or partially as you prefer. This project uses composition metal leaf, rather than real gold, because it is less expensive and easier to work with, and can be antiqued with an aging glaze. Unlike real gold leaf, however, it will tarnish over time if left unvarnished.

TOOLS AND MATERIALS

- Latex gloves
- 3-inch brown painter's masking tape
- Small paintbrush
- Paint tray with liners
- Primer
- Foam brushes
- Paint, satin (use high-gloss if gilding will not be antiqued)
- ½-inch flat synthetic artist's brush
- Water-base or quick-drying oil-base size (adhesive)
- Scissors
- Composition metal leaf
- Mottler (small, soft brush)
- Small stencil brush
- Small container

- Cotton balls
- Paint thinner
- Touchup brush
- ½-inch round nylon artist's brush
- Oil-base varnish or mineral-soluble acrylic varnish, low luster
- Medium (optional), composed of 1 tablespoon linseed oil, 1 tablespoon paint thinner, 2 drops japan drier
- Empty, clean tuna can (optional)
- Artist's oils: cassel earth, burnt umber, Van Dyke brown (optional)
- Artist's palette (optional)
- Chip brush (optional)

Above: **This gold-leafed medallion has been antiqued with an aging glaze. The base coat color match is American Tradition Lacquer Red.**

Left: **Copper, gold, and silver leafing adorn this magnificent moulding, set against sponged-off walls and a stenciled ceiling.**

Color Matches Wall: base coat: American Tradition Rococo Yellow; glazes: (Decorative Effects products): Metal and Patina Glaze Bronze and Translucent Glaze Moss

PROJECT CONTINUES ➡

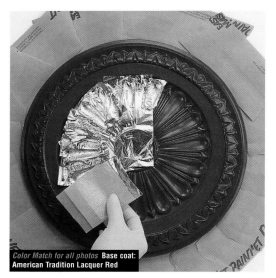

Color Match for all photos **Base coat: American Tradition Lacquer Red**

1 Prepare the surface as directed on pages 184–185. If necessary, mask areas adjacent to the surface that will be gilded. Using a paintbrush, apply primer to the entire surface; let it dry. Then, with a foam brush, apply the base coat, tapping the paint into any crevices and smoothing any bubbles. (We have used Chinese red artist's acrylic as the base paint.) Let the paint dry. Repeat if necessary to achieve full coverage. Remove any tape. With a ½-inch flat artist's brush, apply size to the areas you wish to gild; if you are using oil-base size, apply a thin layer and check that the coverage is even. Be careful not to get size on any adjacent areas. Let the size dry until it's slightly tacky but not sticky—to check, test it lightly with your knuckles, not your finger tips. If you're gilding a relief surface, rather than a flat one, use scissors to cut the leaf into strips slightly longer than the longest contour. Pick up a leaf sandwiched between the tissues it comes in and hold it between your thumb and forefinger.

2 Sliding the bottom tissue out completely, lower the leaf onto the surface. To secure the leaf, pat the top tissue against it with a finger. Continue to apply the leaf, adding each piece so that it slightly overlaps the previous piece. Where there is no size, excess leaf may tear off as you work. You can add the pieces to the surface as you go or set them aside.

LOWE'S QUICK TIP
When applying leaf to a solid area, such as the center of a medallion, begin at the outer edge and work toward the center.

3 Pounce the leafed surface with a mottler to make sure the leaf adheres tightly.

4 Fill any gaps in the leafed area, gently tearing off overhanging pieces and repositioning them with the mottler or your fingers.

5 Use a stencil brush to rub the leaf more tightly onto the surface, and at the same time brush off any loose pieces of leaf, catching them in a small container. If you accidentally put size in an area you didn't want to gild, remove the unwanted leaf with a cotton ball dipped in a little paint thinner.

6 Rub the leafed areas with a dry cotton ball to smooth out any wrinkles. To patch remaining gaps, carefully apply size to them with a touchup brush and let it dry until it's slightly tacky. Then fill the gaps with leaf scraps from the container. Pounce them with the mottler and smooth with a cotton ball. If necessary, touch up the exposed base coat with more paint. Let the gilding dry overnight. Using a round nylon artist's brush, brush around all the relief features to remove any loose bits of metal leaf. Add a coat of low luster varnish to prevent discoloration, or proceed with Step 7.

7 The gilding is now complete and can be left as is if you wish. If you would like to antique it, you can apply an aging glaze to dull the gold and deepen the color of the paint. To do so, mix the medium in a tuna can. Squeeze a small amount of each artist's oil onto a palette. Dip the round nylon artist's brush into the medium, then pick up some of each color and mix on the palette. Brush the glaze over the entire surface, covering the gilded and painted areas completely. If too much glaze accumulates in the relief features or the glaze seems too heavy, you can pounce out the excess with a stencil brush or a chip brush (see page 97 for pouncing). Let the glaze dry. Add a coat of low luster varnish to prevent discoloration.

LOWE'S SAFETY TIP
Spread out oil-soaked rags to dry outdoors or in a well-ventilated area away from pets, children, sparks, and other sources of combustion; do not leave the materials unattended overnight. Dispose of the materials according to local ordinances.

lacquered box

LACQUERWARE STANDS OUT IN ANY decor. The labor-intensive process of coating items in many layers of black and red lacquers actually dates back to the New Stone Age in China. You can duplicate this stunning effect with far less effort using the faux lacquer technique shown here. Try it on boxes, tabletops, wood bowls, or other decorative elements you'd like to use as color accents in a room. As you finish your work on the project each day, clean up with paper towels or rags and prepare additional medium and paint as needed.

TOOLS AND MATERIALS

- Wood box
- Latex primer, brown (if necessary)
- Sandpaper (320-grit)
- Tack cloth
- Latex gloves
- Alkyd paint, satin, red-orange
- Paint tray with liners
- 1- and 2-inch flat artist's brushes
- Artist's oils (for red lacquer): alizarin crimson, burnt umber
- Medium, composed of 1 tablespoon linseed oil, 1 tablespoon paint thinner
- Mineral spirits
- Mixing containers
- Stirring sticks
- Japan drier
- Cotton-knit rags
- Stippling brush or 2-inch paintbrush
- Polyurethane varnish, gloss
- Gold powder or paint

A box finished with a faux-lacquer treatment is an attractive accessory for a desk or coffee table—or an elegant, and relatively simple, gift.

1 Prepare the box as directed on pages 184–185, removing any hardware. If necessary, prime the box, applying two coats if you need to for good coverage. Sand and wipe with a tack cloth after each coat. Faux lacquer must be painted over a very smooth surface, so it is preferable to use an alkyd paint for your base coat. Apply the base coat with a 2-inch artist's brush, stroking in the direction of the grain; let a bit of the primer show through. Let the base coat dry.

2 Mix equal amounts (roughly, ⅙ cup of each) of the alizarin crimson artist's oil, the medium, and mineral spirits to make ½ cup of glaze. It should be the consistency of thick cream. In a different container, mix the burnt umber artist's oil the same way. Add a few drops of japan drier (3 drops of drier to ½ cup of glaze) to each color.

3 Using a 1-inch flat artist's brush, dab the red glaze onto the box, leaving big gaps, so that it covers a total of about 75 percent of the box. Move across the box in the direction of the grain as you dab on the glaze. Dip a clean flat brush in the brown glaze and fill in the gaps with dabs of glaze, again working in the direction of the grain.

4 Blend the two colors together by pouncing (see page 97) a cotton rag smoothed over a wad of rags over the surface. With a stippling brush or paintbrush, stipple on red glaze so that there are no brush marks left visible (see pages 145–147). Let the finish dry completely.

5 With the 1-inch flat artist's brush, apply a coat of varnish, stroking in the direction of the grain. Sand lightly and wipe with a tack cloth. To achieve a sparkling effect, add gold powder or paint to the varnish and apply to the box. Let the varnish dry completely. Reattach the hardware.

LOWE'S QUICK TIP

You can use a hair dryer to speed the drying.

credits

DESIGN

10: Sandra C. Watkins and Joan Osburn/Osburn Design; Mark McMahon and Mark Dillon/Chameleon Fine Painting

11 top: Bauer Interior Design

13 right: Joe P. Carr, Texture Antiques

15 left: Josefina Larrain and Salvador Reyes; right: Dominic Mercadante, AIA

17: Joel Hendler and Christopher Pollock/Hendler Design

18: Studio Roshambeau

19 top: Louis Butler/Butler Armsden Architects; Osburn Design; bottom: City Studios

20 bottom: Burks Toma Architects

21 top: Agnes Bourne; bottom: Randall Whitehead (lighting design)

22: James McCalligan

23 top: Gigi Rogers Designs; bottom: Freddy Moran

24 top: Markie Nelson

25 top: John Knudson, Knudson Gloss Architects; bottom: Ann Jones

26 top: Paul Wanzer (architecture), Kim Munizza (design)

29 top: Alla Kazovsky/Kids, Studio; bottom: Loretta Gargan Landscape + Design

30 bottom left: Royce Meyerott and Lee Bryant

31 top: Brad Polvorosa, Neos (design), Nova Designs (builder); bottom: Janice Stone Thomas, ASID, CKD, Stone-Wood Design, Inc.

32: Denise Foley Design and David Brewster

33 top: Lucianna Samu Design; bottom: Markie Nelson

34 top: Marlene Rochon (design), Jon Pearce Designs (painting)

35: Lilley Yee Interiors, Suzanne Mastroluca

36: Millie Anne Koomas Design

37: The Beardsley Company

38 top: George Constant Interiors

39 bottom: Charles de Lisle/Your Space, Inc. (design), Willem Racké (painting)

42 right: Philip J. Meyer, Ltd., Shirley Robinson Painted Finishes

43 bottom: Angela Caverly

44 top: Jan Kavale; bottom: Brad and Katy Polvorosa, Neos

45 left: Steven Goldstein; right: Kathleen Navarra/Navarra Design Consultants

46: Katie White, ASID

47 left: Deborah Morant; right: Ralph E. A. Frischman

48 right: Croworks of Marin

49 left: Millie Anne Koomas Design; right: Denise Foley Design and David Brewster

50: Gail Whiting Design Consultants

51: Janice McCabe/McCabe & Sommers Interiors

52 top: Robert Orr

53 top: Robert Mintum Coale/Old World Finishes; bottom: Alejandro Patrón

55: Gail Lesley Diehl Interiors

56 top: Robert O'Connor Designs (painting); bottom: Jeffrey Becom and Sally Jean Aberg

57 top right: Jan Kavale; bottom: Linda Applewhite & Associates

61: CJ Designs

67: Gary Lord/Gary Lord Wall Options

68: Bauer Interior Design

70: Jim Davis

105 top: Sarah Caska

105 center and bottom, 106 bottom, 118–119, 120 right, 121, 126–127, 134–135, 181, 190–191: Dede Lee, art direction and painting

106 top: Freddy Moran and Carlene Anderson Kitchen Design

107 top: Jeanese Rowell, Design, Richard Ford and Abel Fuentas (painting); bottom: Dennis Welch-May

108 left: Charlotte Jensen and Associates; right: Susan Churcher

109 top: Sasha Emerson Design Studio; bottom: James Shay, architect

110: Annie Cronin and Maria Quinby (design), Lisa Atoji and Janet Costa (painting)

111: Custom Design by Melissa & Mary

112: Philip J. Meyer, Ltd., Shirley Robinson Painted Finishes

114 left: Claudia Blaine

115: Debbie Schwartz/The Village Collection

116–117: Bill Samios

120 left: Lilley Yee Interiors, Suzanne Mastroluca (painting)

140: Tucker & Marks

141 left: Studio Roshambeau

142 bottom, 143 left, 146 bottom, 147 bottom left, center, right, bottom, 148–149, 151–154, 157, 159, 160 top left and right, 162–163, 170, 172–173, 177 top, 178 bottom, 179, 192 bottom left and right, 193, 195, 199, 201–208, 209 top, 210–211, 212 left, 213–214, 215 top, 216–217: Justina Jorrin Barnard/Peinture Decorative

143 right: Jeff Lincoln Interiors, Inc.

158: Hearst Specials

170–171: Gary Lord/Gary Lord Wall Options

177 bottom: Philip J. Meyer, Ltd., Shirley Robinson Painted Finishes

178 top: Stephanie Stokes

180 left: Marlene Rochon (design), Jon Pearce Designs (painting)

186–187: Erik Seniska

188–189: Jil Peters; Takashi Katano, courtesy of Kawade Shobo Shinsha Publishers

196–197: Peter O. Whiteley

198 top: Jeanese Rowell, Design, Richard Ford and Abel Fuentas (painting); bottom: Charles Spada

200: Flegel's Home Furnishings

209 bottom: Shelley Masters

212 right: Frank Van Duerm Design Associates, Samantha Renko (painting)

215 bottom: Robert O'Conner Designs (painting)

218–219: Jon Pearce Designs (painting)

PHOTOGRAPHY

Russell Abraham, 56 bottom; **Patrick Barta,** 43 top; **Caroline Bureau, Robert Chartier, Michel Thibaut,** 130–131, 155–156; **James Carrier,** 105 top right, 188, 189 top right and right; **Todd Caverly/Brian Vanden Brink,** 43 bottom; **Glenn Cormier,** 108 left; **Mark Darley/ESTO,** 140; **Phillip H. Ennis,** 38 top, 50, 215 bottom; **Everett & Soulé,** 14, 26 bottom; **Cheryl Fenton,** 34 top, 35–36, 39 bottom, 49 left, 105 left center, right center, left bottom, right bottom, 106 bottom, 107 top, 110, 114–115, 118–121, 126–127, 134–135, 177 bottom, 180–181, 190–191, 198 top, 218–219; **Ron Forth,** 67, 170–171; **Tria Giovan,** 47 left, 192 top left, 194; **John Granen,** 24 top, 26 top, 33 bottom; **Ken Gutmaker,** 17 top, 42 left, 45 left, 57 bottom; **Jamie Hadley,** 10, 23 top, 42 right, 44 bottom, 45 right, 47 right, 55, 84 left, 90 top, 109 top, 112, 186, 187 top and bottom left; **John M. Hall,** 145 top, 178 top; **Philip Harvey,** 19 top, 48 right, 185 bottom, 200, 209 bottom; **Scott Hirko,** 12, 20 top, 41, 59, 73–75, 78 top, 80–82, 85, 90 bottom, 103, 139, 183; **Muffy Kibbey,** 20 bottom; **Dennis Krukowski,** 143 right; **David Livingston,** 104; **Tim Maloney,** 30 bottom left; **Steven Mays,** 37, 76–77, 83, 88–89, 91, 98–99, 142 bottom, 143 left, 146 bottom, 147 bottom left, top right, center, and bottom, 148–149, 151–154, 157, 159, 160 top and right, 162–163, 170, 172–173, 177 top, 178 bottom, 179, 187 bottom right, 192 bottom left and right, 193, 195, 199, 201–208, 209 top, 210–211, 212 left, 213–214, 215 top, 216–217; **E. Andrew McKinney,** 11 top, 18, 19 bottom, 22, 23 bottom, 28 bottom, 29 top, 32, 39 top, 49 right, 51, 56 top, 57 top left, 78 bottom, 106 top, 109 bottom, 141 left, 212 right; **Geoffrey Nilsen,** 30 top; **Eric O'Connell,** 108 right; **Robert Perron,** 52 top, 53 top, 107 bottom; **David Phelps,** 70; **Kenneth Rice,** 13 left, 21; **Eric Roth,** 198 bottom; **Mark Samu,** 33 top, 38, 61, 111, 158; **Sibila Savage,** 29 bottom; **Michael Skott,** 54, 63; **Thomas J. Story,** 68, 116–117, 196–197; **E. Spencer Toy,** 189 top left and bottom; **Cheryl Ungar,** 25 top; **Brian Vanden Brink,** 15 right; **Christopher Vendetta,** 84 right, 86–87; **David Wakely,** 25 bottom, 31, 44 top, 48 left, 57 top right; **Jessie Walker,** 46, 160 bottom left; **Karen Witynski,** 13 right, 15 left, 53 bottom; **Tom Wyatt,** 185 top

ILLUSTRATION

Beverley Bozarth Colgan, 9, 14, 92–95, 174, 176 left; **Robert Greisen,** 96–97, 176 right, 180; **Randy Miyake,** 122–125, 128–129

index